Finding My Way

Finding My Way

Facing My Journey With Courage

With companion workbook and exercises

Donna Markussen

ISBN: 1543115217
ISBN 13: 9781543115215
Library of Congress Control Number: 2017902518
CreateSpace Independent Publishing Platform
North Charleston, South Carolina

Acknowledgments

I WOULD LIKE to say a special thank you to my husband Steve, and my two sons Billy and Taylor, I am so grateful to have you in my life.

Lynette Benton, my early editor, for inspiring me to start my writing and motivating me to keep the process going.

Michelle Roccia, my loving sister-in-law, for believing in me.

Sarah Lovett, my writing coach, whose guidance and feedback improved my writing style.

Cynde Christie, my editor and coach, who challenged me throughout my writing process and offered honest feedback and support. Her high-energy and willingness to explore with me was a gift.

Deborah Morningstar, reader, offering constructive feedback and insight that helped me bring more depth to my story.

Diane Guernsey, reader, helping me explore areas of my manuscript that needed more clarity and vision.

PREFACE

Embracing The Tapestry Of Our Lives

*"Life can only be understood backwards,
but it must be lived forwards"*

…. SOREN KIERKEGAARD

As I SIT in my beautiful lake house, overlooking the majestic mountains of New Hampshire, taking in the beauty of all the pine, maple and birch trees, enjoying birds of different colors and sizes, perching and singing on those trees, I feel a sense of inner peace. This place I call home is often referred to as *God's Country*. As I write this, I am able to contemplate how lucky and grateful I am for having such a wonderful life.

It wasn't always that way

"Why would you want to expose your life in a book? You have to be crazy to do that. No one wants to go back and revisit all the shit that happened to them." My husband, Steve, graciously reminded me. He had a valid point. But, I kept asking myself, "Am I going to make a difference in someone's life by exposing my own truth?" I finally got my answer and that is when I began my writing.

This book will take you on my journey and its purpose is an open invitation for you to reflect on your own journey and to help you find the many lessons you may have yet to find.

My story starts with growing up with family members with mental illness. It will seem depressing and dark at first, but you will soon see the significance it played in my life as a young child.

The examples and stories in this book are my own personal struggles and how through them I opened up to find a better way, whether that was changing my inner belief system, finding people who inspired me to grow, or educating myself to help me get through a serious health condition.

Each story's purpose is not to spill my heart and soul out as a memoir, it is to demonstrate by example how I was able to *learn* and *grow* through each challenge, navigating my way out of the madness, out of pain and suffering, out of emotional self-sabotage, out of depression and disease.

It was as if each time a challenging person or issue appeared in my life, I approached it like hitting a baseball. Each time that ball (challenge) was heading towards me, I found a way to hit it back out into the field. In baseball, sometimes you hit the ball, sometimes you miss. In my life, most of the time, I missed. The point of my story is that I got back up and tried again.

I believe there is an intelligence within us all that is always guiding us towards the path that will bring us inner peace. It's having a determination, an inner knowing, to tap into that intelligence and believing that you have what it takes to survive the mess that is going on in your life at this moment. Some people choose to listen to this early in their lives, for some it takes years. And for some, they need a little nudging, a little guidance, to start the ball rolling. That is the purpose of this book.

I believe all of our challenges teach us to be a better (and stronger) version of ourselves. We go from feeling like "this shouldn't have happened to me," which keeps us locked inside our own emotional prison, to opening up our hearts, and asking, "What have I learned from all of this?" We grow into a stronger, more resilient person. Having that awareness helps us approach life with confidence in our ability to work through challenging times.

Too many people who can't see their own worth, their own intelligence, their own value have wasted their lives. They numb themselves and live on autopilot letting others make important decisions for them. This happens most when it comes to our health. We believe that our only option is to listen to the doctor's advice, take a pill, and we're supposed to feel better. However, when we don't feel better by doing what we've been told to do, we blame ourselves. We believe our poor health is our fate, and we give up, as we let disease win, without investigating it further.

I hope by reading this book, you will begin to investigate and be open to changing your current perspective. I hope you learn to question everything you have accepted into your reality that's not working and ask yourself, "Is there something more I can do that is going to help me find a better way?"

If there is one challenge in this book that motivates you to make a change, then I have done my job. That may be investigating a new job, or career, or deciding to stop letting other people walk all over you. Maybe you look into alternative medicine for that auto-immune disease you have been living with, or you decide it's time to take care of your body, mind and soul with good nutrition, quiet time, and daily exercise. These are all good choices make one for yourself!

When we start to listen to our inner guidance, we will receive more information that will help us reach that place that we all desire – health, happiness and inner peace.

In Part 5 of this book, I have included a companion workbook to help you work through that process. I hope you take full advantage of it!

Table of Contents

PART ONE

Waking Up

"To be nobody-but-yourself in a world which is doing its best, night and day, to make you everybody but yourself – means to fight the hardest battle which any human being can fight – and never stop fighting. 'Staying real' is one of the most courageous battles that we'll ever fight.

---E.E. CUMMINGS

CHAPTER 1

"The most powerful weapon on earth
is the human soul on fire."

---MARSHAL FERDINAND FOCH

THIS IS A book about *courage*. Courage to show up and be seen, and *own your truth* regardless of what other people think, say or do. Courage to listen to and trust the inner *wisdom* that is always guiding us, yet most often we ignore it. It is about the courage to face our fears, perceived limitations, insecurities, and unworthiness, and charge forward anyway, with grace. Courage to *dismantle* all of our old stories, limiting beliefs, self-sabotaging habits and unconscious behaviors that keep us stuck in the past, tightly woven in a blanket of shame, pain and guilt. And courage to set boundaries by placing limits on people that try to overpower our lives and take a stand by saying "No" instead of "Yes" in order to respect ourselves without guilt or fear. Instead, we find the courage to wake up to our own magnificence, the good, the bad and the ugly, while sharing ourselves with the world. We move away from all the darkness into our light.

This book is also about the many challenges we face in our lives, and the lessons we can learn from those challenges. It is about getting to know our *whole* self, which includes our dark side as well as our light. Every painful situation that showed up in my life helped me to realize more about my place in this world and myself.

Most of my youth I wanted to just blend in and go unnoticed, feeling unworthy to receive anything more than what I believed I deserved. I coddled my inner shame and insecurities like a baby, and I always found ways to prove that my misguided beliefs about myself were true to others as well as to myself.

The Early Years, Choosing Light Over Darkness

My self-sabotaging habits and unconscious behaviors were rooted from my childhood experiences and my beliefs about myself. Growing up with family members who suffered from mental illness was scary and confusing. It started with my Nana, my mother's maternal mother. Nana tried to commit suicide several times throughout her life. The first time I realized this was when I was 12 years old. I came home from school to find my mother lying in bed, sobbing uncontrollably with bloodshot eyes. When I asked my father why mom was so upset, he replied,

"Nana tried to commit suicide *again*."

"*Again?*" I thought. I didn't realize then that this was "normal" behavior for my grandmother. My two older brothers and I barely knew our Nana. She was not the warm and fuzzy grandmother, who made visits with open arms full of hugs and kisses. Her visits were the complete opposite. She was only 4'9" tall, with white silver hair. However, her size carried a chilling presence, as if you were facing a formidable iceberg. Her glaring eyes always penetrated deep inside me. The chill in the air was evidence that danger was ahead. The awkward silence in the room was an eerie message for me to leave immediately. Both my parents kept quiet about her mental illness and the many haunting details of it, wanting to shield us from the darkness and to protect our innocence.

My grandmother had suffered years of sadness and clinical depression, probably for her whole life. Her husband, my grandfather, became an alcoholic, self-medicating to help numb his dark reality. In those days, doctors didn't have the many mood stabilizers and medications we have available today. At that time, the stigma of living with mental illness was considered one of the most humiliating, and misunderstood diseases. People would gossip in mock horror while rolling their eyes in disgrace. To survive that embarrassment, you would do everything you could to keep it a secret from the outside world.

My only memories of visiting my maternal grandparents' home are dim, but I know that as soon as I arrived I wanted to leave. I would get an eerie feeling in the pit of my stomach. When I visited, no matter how hard I tried, I could not shake that feeling. Their house was immaculate, stark looking and felt cold, void of life, void of emotion, void of love. I can't imagine how my mother dealt with that darkness as a little girl growing up. I didn't know it then, but that was my first intuitive nudge speaking to me, telling me something wasn't right.

That day I came home from school was not the first time I witnessed my mother in a profound state of sadness. There were times she would go for days sequestered in her bedroom, self-medicating with prescription drugs, including tranquilizers, painkillers and anti-depressants, while coping with profound sadness brought on by her chemical imbalance and a longing to connect with her own mother. At the time, I was not aware of the details behind her sorrow, but knew it had something to do with my Nana. I just clung to the hope that she would feel better soon. If she wasn't retreating, her behavior was unpredictable and even scary at times. As a small child, I didn't have the skills to comprehend the meaning behind her sadness or her physical outbursts.

My mother was the oldest of four children; she took over the parenting role of bringing up her three younger siblings while their mother was emotionally detached dealing with her inner demons. Looking back, I can't imagine the horror of her daily life, as both parents were unpredictable and disconnected. Mom had to navigate her daily life on her own, suppressing her own fears and emotions to survive, at the same time assuming the parenting role of her three younger siblings not by choice, but by default.

All of her suppressed emotions and fears lay buried deep inside her subconscious and were the source of my mother's chronic high anxiety "fight or flight" response to simple things that most people would take in stride. She was a perfectionist, and everything she did, including keeping the house clean and in order, was paramount. Faithfully, every Saturday, she and my father would dedicate the whole day to cleaning our small home. I used to tell her that she was not killing the germs she was annihilating them! Her need for perfection meant if anyone left a glass on a table, or dishes in the sink, or a shirt lying around, she would go into a screaming fit, throwing shoes and punching walls that left permanent holes. This was a response mechanism, learned as a child, dealing with her mother's mental illness, to keep order as best as she could. All of her fearful thoughts and behaviors stayed with her as she grew into an adult. She programmed her subconscious to react in a way that would self-inflict pain in her body.

The inside of our bathroom door was a daily reminder of those outbursts with a huge dent from the force of her fist. I always knew when I heard her scream "*Jesus Christ!*" that immediately following would be a tsunami of slamming doors and cabinets, or throwing anything that she could find in her wake, along with yelling and screaming. Similar to the warning we all heed as soon as lightning strikes. We brace ourselves for the eruption of the rumbling thunders and heavy rain. The eruption my mother produced would create an enormous amount of stress in my stomach and I would immediately retreat to my room, close the door, and wait for her internal storm to be over. I desperately wanted my mother to stop abusing herself this way and longed for her to calm down and be happy. I learned not to say anything, and tried to keep order as best I could to avoid causing any of these outbursts. This taught me that it was *safe* to be quiet. Which gave birth to my belief of my unworthiness, causing a tremendous amount of inner turmoil and shame.

My mother cared about her parents deeply, and longed to have a loving relationship with them. When I became a young adult, I saw that as the years went by, and better treatment options became available, they began to build that wished for loving, sustainable re-lationship. My grandmother received proper medications to help her disease, which helped her live a better quality of life. My grandfather also stopped drinking.

As their relationship mended, our relationship deepened as well. My mother was less stressed and reactive, and was able to live a more heart-centered life. She was able to enjoy her life more. She and my father developed some close friendships, and every Saturday night, my parents looked forward to going out dancing with their friends. They would never miss a Saturday night. That night meant the world to them.

As a young adult, bringing up my two sons, I realized the pro-found pain and sadness my mother endured as a young girl. I was grateful to be able to understand the depth of her illness and suf-fering, and accept her for who she was, without judgment. I was also grateful to have those moments with her later in life, where I would witness her joy. We would have many meaningful conversations and our relationship was more open, as I wasn't living in fear of her self-sabotaging behaviors the way I did in the past.

Visiting Dad's parents was the opposite experience. Grammy and Grandpa always welcomed me with open arms. "God Bless You!" and many kisses always followed hugs from Grammy. Grandpa would play his piano and sing songs. Seeing them made it clear where Dad got his loving and open nature.

When my mother married my father, Dad became the light that was missing from Mom's life. He never had a bad thing to say about anyone. He balanced out my mother's lows with his natural high. When my mother got depressed, Dad was always there to pick up the pieces, patiently waiting for her to feel better, while helping us kids to lead normal lives. Dad was full of loving emotion, and adored his children and his wife. He always made me feel safe and loved. When I was a little girl, we would play a special game. I would sit on his lap, and he would ask me "Whose little girl are you?" I knew if my answer was correct, he would give me lots of hugs and kisses, followed by a rub of his cheek to my cheek. Although sometimes Dad's cheek was scratchy with whiskers, wow did I love it!

Later in life, we would have conversations about my dating life. He would tell me how important it was not to allow any man to try to overpower, take advantage or belittle me. "Don't settle Donna, you deserve better than most of those jerks out there." He would say. He knew firsthand how men could easily sweep you off your feet, using their agenda for casual sex and then move on to the next one. Dad was a player in his day, literally and figuratively. In his youth, he played left fielder for a semi-pro baseball league. He was extremely handsome and had women falling at his feet. With his charming personality and looks, it was easy to see why. He broke many hearts back then, but the day he met my mother all that was history. I listened to his advice and as a result found my perfect part-ner, and have been happily married for 35 years. My father's compas-sion and lightheartedness, gave me the desire to choose to focus my attention in the same direction. My wanting to hold onto that light regardless of what obstacle or horrific life event appeared propelled me to investigate and pursue my own truth.

The Unpredictability Of Living With Mental Illness

My mother's younger sister, Diane, was my favorite aunt. I always got excited to see her when she came for a visit and she was just as excited to see me. Aunt Diane led an exciting life, at least I believed that at the time, and she would show up at random times, unannounced, ready to party. Sometimes we would not see her for months or years at a time; however, when she came, she was full of high energy, bear-ing many gifts for everyone. It was like waking up on Christmas morning. She was full of laughter, always telling clever jokes, and she had a keen sense of fashion, which I adored. Aunt Diane seemed to me the coolest aunt on this earth.

This was in my early years when my mother was living with clini-cal depression and mood swings, so when my Aunt Diane showed up, I gravitated towards her high energy and spunk. I was her princess and she always gave special attention to me, which made my brothers jealous. I found out later in life that she would manufacture stories to tell my parents to get my brothers into trouble. I was blind to this as I was too busy having a good time when I was in her pres-ence. She was my escape from dealing with my mother's fear and sad-ness. We would take frequent day trips on the train, visiting exciting Boston landmarks like the Boston Commons, Filenes Basement, The Prudential Center, Old Iron Sides and many more. I loved our trips together as I never experienced this kind of adventurous fun with my mother. She would not travel outside of our own city. It was always an adventure with Aunt Diane. I was grateful to have her in my life.

One day, Aunt Diane disappeared from our lives, as was her custom. I could not understand why and my parents just said she needed time to work out her life. Then, as she had done in the past, she reappeared at our house unannounced. This time she was with her latest boyfriend, Paul, and their toddler daughter Lisa, who was two years old. Lisa was like a little angel, with the cutest round face and button nose, with brunette hair. It was love at first sight for me.

I was happy Aunt Diane was back in my life, and her new family lived close by in Chelsea. The four of us would take day trips, visiting campgrounds in Maine, where we would have picnics, go swimming, and enjoy each other's company. I felt as though Lisa was my baby sister and I completely adored her. During the school week, I wanted Lisa in my life as much as possible. I made sure I was available after school and I would quickly come home and we would go to the playground or play games outside such as hide and seek together.

Then, suddenly, Aunt Diane began acting very strange. She was confused, delusional and extremely anxious. I couldn't comprehend what was happening. My parents explained to me that Aunt Diane was living with a condition called *Bi-Polar Disorder.**

*Bi-Polar Disorder, formerly called manic depression, causes extreme mood swings that include emotional highs (mania or hypomania) and lows (depression). When you become depressed, you may feel sad or hopeless and lose interest or pleasure in most activities. When your mood shifts in the other direction, you may feel euphoric and full of energy. Mood shifts may occur only a few times a year or as often as several times a week. *Mayo Clinic

Living with manic highs and debilitating lows is exhausting. When her mood was up, she was flying high on life, it's then when my aunt always showed up at our house; however when she was down, she was so low she became incapable of functioning. Hallucinating and living in a delusional world can become the norm. Aunt Diane's illness took a toll on her relationship with Paul, and they split up.

I was anxiously waiting to hear from my parents where my aunt and Lisa would live. Thankfully, my parents considered it best that they stay with us for a while as Aunt Diane figured things out. This was for a period of about two years. Because of Aunt Diane's condition, my parents were always on high alert, understanding her illness was unpredictable. They never knew how her Bi-Polar personality would manifest from one day to the next. I witnessed this firsthand one Saturday morning when my parents received a phone call from the Chelsea police reporting that they picked up my aunt. Aunt Diane had been down at the local playground running in circles screaming obscenities.

The reality of her illness struck me hard. As I became aware of my aunt's mental illness, I was able to witness the devastation it caused. Lisa was too young to realize what was going on with her mother, but her actions told us, she was frightened. She always came to my parents and me for comfort. We realized how important it was to provide Lisa with consistency and to feel safe, something her mother could not provide. We took over every aspect of her daily life to ensure that. But, things progressively got worse. One morning, my aunt was in such a state of rage, her eyes bulging, talking incessantly almost as if she was possessed, while holding Lisa in her hands. I froze in horror as I witnessed what she was about to do. "Get her, Bob!!!" I heard my mother yell to my father. In Aunt Diane's delusional state, she was about to throw Lisa down the basement stairs!

11

My father took swift action, reached out, and snatched Lisa from her grasp, taking her just in the nick of time.

That day, my parents decided it was time to get my aunt out of the house and into a hospital for treatment for her illness with proper medication and psychiatric care. They contacted her social worker (apparently, she'd had one all along, living with her BI-Polar disorder) and arranged to get her into a hospital that day.

Lisa is like a baby sister to me. I wanted to protect her. It only made sense after what happened that my parents would consider adopting her. The next day, when I went to school, The Department of Social Services swiftly came and took Lisa (with my parent's consent) out of our house. When I came home, Lisa was gone. I ran from room to room trying to find her. Then I began to panic as I realized what had happened. My parents explained that they (with the advice of Social Services) thought Lisa would be better off not living in our home. I couldn't believe what I was hearing. I screamed and yelled at them, then cried. I was so angry. "You took her while I was in school!" I yelled. They explained that the purpose was to shield me from the pain. But, it didn't. I cried so much for weeks and months after losing Lisa. That was the saddest day of my life.

It wasn't until years later, as I became a young adult and the mother of my two sons that I realized the magnitude of what my parents went through with their agonizing decision to let Lisa go. If they had kept Lisa, Aunt Diane would freely come in and out of her daughter's life, showing up at our house, at random times, causing havoc in all of our lives. Letting Lisa go was the most selfless choice they could have made. It was a chance for Lisa to live a normal life, away from the chaos, away from the mental illness.

I now realize my parents chose love over fear. This is the power of *choice*. My parents chose to stop the madness, even though it caused them a tremendous amount of pain and suffering of their own. And, they also had to live with the pain and suffering it caused their own family, especially me. Looking back, that must have been torture. Letting Lisa go was an act of *courage*, one that would offer hope to all of us. They took responsibility and decided they would not allow another person's actions to dictate how they would live their lives.

Their love for Lisa and my aunt, made their choice possible. Had they been stuck in playing the *story* over and over in their minds of how *guilty* they would feel letting Lisa go, separating her from her own mother, things would have been different. Guilt holds us stuck in the past, leaving us powerless. We deny our ability to access our own inner guidance, our intuition. My parents both chose to listen to their intuition and let Lisa go, knowing that it was her best chance. I'm not saying they didn't feel sad, because they did, but Mom had taken care of her baby sister all her life, and realized the magnitude of Diane's illness. She stood by the decision with power and conviction

This is a prime example of taking responsibility for anything life throws at you. They didn't blame my grandparents, Aunt Diane or themselves. That would have kept them paralyzed and incapable of moving forward. Instead, they chose to stay in their power, take swift action, trusting in their decision, regardless of how painful their *sacrifice* was. *They were giving Lisa her best chance at a healthy life.*

The next generation of mental illness began with my older brother Bobby's diagnosis of Schizophrenia when he was a young man. That was a terrifying and heartbreaking time in my life. It was through Bobby's illness that I learned a great deal about myself.

CHAPTER 2

Growing Up With Mental Illness In My Own Generation

*Accept the challenges to which fate binds you. You will
learn a great deal about yourself through them.*

IT WAS THE week before Christmas in 2012. I walked into my brother, Bobby's group home with two big bags full of gifts. He had called me in November to let me know what he wanted for Christmas.

"I need socks," he said.

"That's it?" I asked.

"And underwear," he continued.

I laughed because I knew I was going to surprise him with much more.

After I arrived at his group home, Bobby opened his gifts, and his gaze was wide with anticipation and appreciation for each item he held up. "I'm all set Donna," he said. "Thank you! I am so happy you remembered!"

The gift bags I'd brought were full of socks, underwear, shirts, sweatshirts, pants and boots, with a few gift cards thrown in from Dunkin' Donuts and McDonald's. There were also a few lottery scratch cards he loved playing the scratch cards.

Bobby is a diagnosed schizophrenic. He fell prey to the disease around the age of 19 after graduating from high school. Up until that age, Bobby was a normal, happy kid, going to school, playing cards, touch football and basketball pickup games. He is the oldest of us three kids, three years older than I am.

When I was 17, Bobby asked if he could borrow my car to go into Boston. I was just noticing that he was starting to act strangely, talk incessantly about religion, carrying a bible with him wherever he went and citing psalms aloud. That day, he wanted to visit Park Street Church in downtown Boston. I agreed, and handed him my car keys. When he came home that afternoon, it was without my car.

"Bobby, where's my car?" I asked him.

He gave me a confused look, and said, "I don't know."

"Bobby!" I yelled. "What do you mean you don't know?"

"I took the train home," he said.

"Bobby, where did you put my car?" I asked again. Hoping I would get another answer.

This time his stare had this dazed, lost look, he truly did not remember taking my car into Boston.

"Oh my God! What is wrong with you?" I yelled.

I ran in the other room and told my parents and they both looked at each other then gave me a look that showed how concerned they were. Suspecting that his personality was changing drastically, they had noticed that Bobby was getting obsessed with religion, and becoming more introverted each day. My mom asked my other brother, David to go and retrieve the car that Bobby had left parked in Boston; luckily, it was still there.

Bobby became more isolated, and began hallucinating, talking about the voices in his head. I was frightened, always on guard, as I watched my brother exhibit this psychotic behavior. I began avoiding him because he would corner me in a room, while holding onto the Bible, and stare at me with a wide-eyed look, citing the important revelations of his newfound religion, and how I should believe it too. It felt like he was involved in a cult. By then he was also more belligerent, and would look at me with pure hatred in his eyes whenever I was getting ready to go out with my friends.

"You think you're so cool," he would say. He would be seething, looking at me with contempt.

I began locking my bedroom door, for fear of what he might do to me when he was in this state. My parents were at their wits' end; every time they took him in for an evaluation with a doctor, Bobby would act normal, and the doctor said he was just going through a phase.

Mental illness runs in our family, and my mother instinctively knew something was wrong, she just didn't know what. Then one day, Bobby lunged at my parents, his eyes bulging, in a state of rage. While he attacked my father, my mother called 911. The police came and removed Bobby from the house. This was a horrible experience for my parents, and it left them shaken, frightened and confused. They later learned that his behavior that day finally enabled Bobby to receive proper help. After his arrest, they placed Bobby in a psych ward at the local hospital, and because of the severity of his disease, the officials referred Bobby to McLean Hospital in Belmont, Massachusetts. They officially diagnosed him during his stay there.

He remained hospitalized for over three months, while they provided him with psychiatric care and a cocktail of medications to ease his symptoms. This was a huge relief for our family, knowing he was finally getting appropriate care. When we visited, I was relieved to be able to carry on a conversation with Bobby again, and saw that things were going to get better.

Bobby's drift into mental illness was a very sad time for our family. I was heartbroken as I watched my brother lose his identity, transforming into a completely different person. I struggled with this for many years, and was fearful and ashamed of what other people would think. I was only in my late teens and early 20's at the time, so I wasn't yet connected to my heart's wisdom. I only saw there was a dark side to my family, and I wanted to hide it from outsiders. I was taking Bobby's diagnosis personally, as if it meant there was something wrong with *me*. At that time in my life, I struggled with my self-worth, so Bobby's illness just added to that burden.

Living A Simple, Happy Life

Bobby is now 58 years old, and is living a happy life. Bobby knows how serious his mental health disability is and how dangerous it would be if he stopped taking his medications. He has slipped a few times. The last time, he befriended a few drug dealers, who stole all of his money and clothes and left him alone on the streets. That was a scary lesson. He now understands if he wants to continue to live a quality life, he needs to stay on schedule with his medications, and stay away from bad people. He is learning to take responsibility for himself.

Bobby's group home has around-the-clock care to help him stay on track. He is happy and grateful for simple things like a place to live, a comfortable bed to sleep in, warm meals, a TV so he won't miss Red Sox games, and meaningful conversations with friends and staff in the group home. He loves going to his day program that he attends a few days a week. He is aware of his disability, but he doesn't place blame or feel like he's a victim. He is genuinely happy for everything that is in his life.

When I listen to Bobby's perspective on life, I am taken aback by how enlightened he is, even though he doesn't realize it. Maybe it's just that I'm realizing that we all have a choice in life, and Bobby chose peace.

Opening Up To Grace

The purpose of sharing Bobby's story is to show us what life truly means—and what matters. This brings up several important questions. Are we truly living life according to our purpose? Do we love those we care about without judgment? Do we take joy and gratitude in the simple pleasure of life?

When a loved one suffers with mental illness, a disease or a disability that prohibits them from fully functioning in a way our society dictates as "normal," this can cause a huge disturbance in our lives as we face the unknown. When I was young, I saw my brother's illness through a lens clouded by fear. I was unable to face his new reality with an open mind. From this experience, I learned that when we can accept the situation for what it is and find the hidden gift that is behind a loved one's disability, we open our hearts up to grace. We learn many valuable lessons through their life's challenges.

Bobby's disability taught me many lessons, and opened my heart up to feelings of compassion, empathy, kindness, patience and acceptance. It's important to be aware of the *meaning* behind our challenges in order to *grow* through them. This is just another step we need to take as we move towards reaching our highest self.

CHAPTER 3

Paying Attention To Your Inner Guidance System

You have the power to change the course
of your life at any given moment

LOOKING BACK AT my life, it amazes me that I ended up having the courage to try new things with such ease. As a child and teenager, I was very insecure, which stemmed from my experiences as a young child, and by my belief that it was safer to be quiet than to speak up. Those limiting beliefs became the foundation of my lack of self-awareness and self-confidence. I always viewed others as being more intelligent than I was, and less damaged, as they did not have the same family issues that I had. I never did well in school because I did not have the confidence that I needed. One of my favorite quotes by Henry Ford says it all...

"Whether you believe you can or whether you believe you cannot,
you will always be right."

Although my fears as a child kept me from trying new things, I now realize how different my life would have been if I'd had a mentor to guide me earlier in life, to talk to me about the possibilities I could reach for.

My brother David, who is one year older than me, was "the smart one" in the family. He was a well-rounded kid, with good grades, active in sports, football and basketball, a good-looking guy, with many friends. He seemed to have it all. My parents wanted to give him the best opportunity they could at the time, so they sent him to a private Catholic high school, Pope John, in Everett, Massachusetts. David did well there, made many friends, continued to play sports, continued to get good grades and then went on to college at the University of Massachusetts in Boston.

The year was 1976, and it was time for me to enter high school. My parents wanted to give me the same opportunities that David had. I resisted the idea at first, but they insisted that I try. I felt I could never live up to the expectations of my older brother, so I went to the private Catholic high school, and acted out in fear. I played it cool, blended in, went along with the flow, but each day before school, I would numb myself, standing outside in a secluded corner of the building smoking marijuana to help erase my fear of people learning about me. Eventually, one of the nuns caught me outside smoking a joint.

"Come over here young lady!" she yelled. "I'm going to call your parents and let them know exactly what you're up to. You should be ashamed of yourself!"

She called my parents, and I was given the "If you don't smarten up, you're going to get kicked out of school!" speech.

I did not smarten up. My grades were poor because I didn't believe that I was worthy of being at the school, so I didn't even try. I made it through half of my freshman year. I proved to myself and everyone else, including my parents, that I didn't belong. Consequently, I transferred to the local public high school, in Chelsea, Massachusetts. Although I made some great friends there, I still had my negative inner dialog and fears, and I continued to self-medicate with alcohol and drugs.

Looking back, I am grateful I made it through this period and lived. I somehow knew I had an emotional "set-point" when it came to playing with drugs and alcohol. In other words, I knew if I went beyond a certain point, I would be swimming in dangerous territory. I witnessed others go down that rabbit hole and it scared the life out of me. Deep down, I didn't want that experience. My pain threshold was not strong enough to go there.

After graduating high school, I never even entertained the idea of going off to college; I felt that it was completely out of my reach. So, I did a year of secretarial school instead. I felt becoming a secretary was an attainable goal. After graduating, I landed a job at a highly respected law firm in Boston and began meeting all kinds of people, which opened up new opportunities for me. My soul's first flicker arrived. I detected something inside myself I never knew existed. I watched my co-workers go about their day with integrity and commitment, and I wanted that, too. My high-school years were behind me, and I ceased to feel the need to self-medicate in order to numb my feelings. Now, I was aware of my surroundings and I put a tremendous amount of pride into how I looked, dressed and talked.

In 1981, I met my soon-to-be-husband, Steve. Steve was from Belmont, Massachusetts, an affluent suburb just outside of Boston. Steve grew up in a moderate, two-family home, with his maternal grandmother and aunt living on the top floor, while he, his three brothers, mother and father lived on the first floor. His parents made me feel welcomed in their home. I loved being there so much that at night, instead of my half-hour drive home to Chelsea, I would stay overnight and go to work in the morning from there. In addition, his mother would have breakfast waiting for me when I woke up. She took pleasure in making me feel comfortable. To this day, I adore her welcoming spirit; and how she finds the light in everyone she meets.

Many of Steve's friends came from affluent families, and he was accustomed to a broader experience of life than I was. Steve loved American history, so on our very first date, he took me to The North Bridge, in Concord Massachusetts. This was the site of the first real battle of the American Revolution. The bridge spans the Concord River. I was delighted and astounded by the beauty of it all, and I enjoyed expanding my geographical awareness.

Turning On The Light

As maturity began to set in, and my beliefs about myself were changing, and I had Steve and his family by my side, my inner dialog expanded. I was aware of all the opportunities that surrounded me on a daily basis, and I wasn't going to sabotage myself any more. It was as if I flipped a switch inside myself and turned on the light. I was able to see everything more clearly. I began to understand that when I looked at others and aspired to be like them because they are good examples of what I could become, that's a part of my soul trying to break through to something better. Up until then, I wouldn't let that happen. Knee deep in my beliefs about myself, I looked at others in a way that only proved my faulty perspective. The good news is I was just a *thought* away from changing the story I told myself. I was able to choose to look in the opposite direction from the thoughts that caused me to suffer. When I did this, I began to see my life take a new direction, towards a future of hope. I learned what we see in others stems from what is really in us.

I was making good money as a secretary, which made me feel great. This job changed my perception of *me*. I was out among some heavy hitters, and was yearning to learn everything I could. Long legal documents would cross my desk, and it was my job to proof-read them. I couldn't even pronounce many of the words I read, let alone know their meaning. One day, a senior partner stopped by my desk.

"Excuse me, would you be so kind to retrieve my gavel from my office, and bring it to me in Conference Room B?" he asked.

As the temperature in my body rose to what felt like 110 degrees, sweat running down my forehead, as my face turned a deep shade of purple, I asked, "What is a gavel?"

"What? You don't know what a gavel is! You're working at a law firm, aren't you?" He said, with a stern, smug look of disbelief, while his arms were flapping up and down. It was as if I told him I didn't know what a *duck l*ooked like.

Luckily for me, the office manager was nearby. She overheard our conversation, and saved the day. She always knew how to take care of the young, inexperienced secretaries. Some lawyers were bru-tally mean, and the office manager was always there to pick up the pieces of our crushed egos. She had years of experience dealing with these jerks. They paid us well, but with certain lawyers, it qualified as combat pay considering how some of the girls were mistreated.

Ashamed and humiliated by this attorney's behavior, I knew I needed to smarten up fast. I held onto my Webster's Dictionary at all times, looked up new words every day and memorized their mean-ings, as well as learning to spell them. It was 1980 and computers were not in common use. Most offices used the IBM Selectric type-writers. There was no spell-check back then, as typewriters did not have that function. To correct mistakes, we used White-Out, a liq-uid that covered typed errors. Nevertheless, it was my intention to learn as much as I could. Setting this intention worked. I did so well that I received a promotion to work for one of the senior partners in the firm. This was the beginning of my professional, emotional and spiritual growth spurt. I was changing my belief system about myself without even realizing it.

When we make a decision to change, to better ourselves, an inner force comes forward on our behalf. The events that transpired in my life prove that. I began to meet other secretaries in my office. I had a lot in common with them as they were also trying to better themselves. They became my tribe-of-influence, though I didn't call it that at the time. I was having fun learning, sharing both work and personal stories with these new friends. We often got together outside of work.

As I gained more self-confidence from my legal secretary jobs, I began to feel excited about my future. I came across an ad in the *Boston Globe* business opportunities section for an interior design business. I spent most of my free time reading magazines and books on home decorating, so when I found this ad, I was compelled to investigate. I called the number on the ad, and the following week I met the president of the regional office in Quincy, Massachusetts. She explained to me that this was a national decorating franchise called Decorating Den and they were selling franchise opportunities here in Massachusetts. Decorating Den is a shop-at-home decorating service. People know them by their large colorful vans, stocked with thousands of samples of fabric, wallpaper, blinds, carpet and accessories.

"Wow! Me, running my own business?" I was excited and nervous at the same time. That meant I would be my own boss, so I would be wearing many hats. This was something that was completely new to me. She assured me that with their vigorous and successful training programs, which cover all aspects of the decorating world as well as the business side, I would be prepared to run my business *and* love my job.

The draw to investors buying into this franchise opportunity was the established relationships with over 100 vendors and manufacturers, including products from wall coverings, furniture, and draperies to accessories. Their "buying power" allowed the franchise owner to be competitive with other large design firms.

Steve and I were living in our dream home on the North Shore. I decided to take the plunge and invest in the Decorating Den franchise. We took out a small equity line on our home to cover the cost of my investment. My passion for decorating and my cold-calling approach earned me many top sales awards from the franchise. This was during the building boom in the 1980's. Steve was doing sales for a home insulation company at the time and I would watch how fearless he was when it came to finding new jobs. Instead of waiting around for the phone to ring, he would go to the local town hall and pull building permits. Then he would visit the homeowners or project managers and talk about his products. He would tell them why his product would be a great option for their home. This was a very successful selling method for him. So, when it was time for me to open my business, I followed his template. I would go directly to the homeowner, or building contractor, and strike up a conversation. This enabled me to have a steady flow of business.

Cold calling came easy for Steve but it was completely new to me. I kept a mantra in the back of my mind, "What's the worst that can happen? They say no?" I have to thank Steve for that. He taught me to go after the business I wanted. I grew a lot in this job, and pushed myself to learn and grow as much as I could while stepping out of my comfort zone. This enabled me to learn more about my abilities and myself.

Finding Your Tribe

Life was good. I was *growing* through this adventure while meeting my new tribe-of influence, women who, like me, were starting up their own businesses. As I changed the way I perceived my life, my life changed. My reality changed. I no longer felt like I did in high school.

What we believe to be true alters our reality. If we feel stuck and want to play small, our world will reflect scarcity. We fall into the trap of thinking, "Things just won't work out for me, so why bother?" I would not have had new opportunities show up in my life if I had continued with that old way of thinking.

It works both ways. If we choose to find the hidden nuggets in each opportunity, while gaining self-awareness and listening to our intuition, we will gain a strong desire to succeed as we attract more opportunities and abundance our way. The power is in choosing which way we want to live.

CHAPTER 4

Losing Everything Can Be An Opportunity For Growth

Staying resilient through tough times, not giving up on your dreams is worth the fight

"HOME PRICES NEVER go down" was a quote often spoken by real estate agents in the early 1980's. People were lining up to take the real-estate broker's exam and get in on the action. Housing prices were at their highest and builders had a steady flow of business constructing condominiums and single-family homes to keep up with the demand.

Steve and I got married in 1983, smack in the middle of one of the biggest real estate booms in U.S. history. Our first piece of real estate was a small one-bedroom condominium.

We lived there for a year, and soon we began buying and selling real estate every year or two, making a steady profit. When we found out I was pregnant with our first son Billy, we decided it was time to settle down, so we scoped out land to build our dream home on the North Shore of Massachusetts.

This is when my interior decorating business was in full swing; I was working with homeowners and building contractors. Steve was working in construction sales for a home insulation company. Every night our conversations were full of great stories of how our day had gone. He was going from house to house meeting builders and homeowners and I was, too. It was an exciting time for both of us.

The Real Estate Crash Of The 1980's

Then, in the late 80's to early 90's real estate values plummeted and foreclosures and bankruptcies soared. Increasing mortgage rates were the blame for the bust. My clients were walking away from their home purchases and filing for bankruptcy, which meant I wasn't being paid.

My business' payment policy was a 50% deposit. Final payment was due when the job was finished. Suddenly, I wasn't receiving my final payments. Money was getting scarce. In addition, I had a lot of money tied up in a large project. I was working with a single man named Louie, who was a local contractor. Louie hired me to help with decorating his beautiful custom built home on the North Shore. When the project was completed, I called Louie to set up a time to go over all the details of the decorating project as well as collect the remaining balance due, which was over $10,000.

Louie suddenly disappeared, stopped taking my calls. There was no email back then, so I could only rely on voice mail. Days, then weeks went by and I did not hear back from him, even though I kept calling and leaving messages. I grew nervous and frustrated at the same time, realizing I was going to lose over $10,000 if I could not collect the money he owed me. All of the outstanding balance had to go to the manufacturers and product supply companies that I hired for Louie's job as well as other jobs that were outstanding. That was the only cash flow left in my business. Without it, I would be paying back my business debts from my personal bank account, which due to the economy, was also dwindling.

Steve said to me, "Donna, just go over to his house and wait for him to come home. That's the only way you will know if he's happy with the job or not."

I thought to myself, "Ok, I know what he's saying, but how can *I* possibly manage that?"

In spite of how extremely uncomfortable I was with this idea, out of desperation, I took Steve's advice and decided to go to Louie's house. I parked my van out front, and waited for him to come home from work. When he showed up, I got out of my van to greet him. He pretended that his evasion was an oversight; he was just busy. I didn't want to cause any tension between us, so I went along with his excuse, while I walked with him into his house to collect my final payment. As Steve pointed out, this enabled me to know if Louie was happy or not with my decorating. Turns out, he was very happy with his new space. I walked out with check in hand.

Louie was my very last decorating client. I decided to close the doors of my business before something like this happened again. I knew the next time I may not be as fortunate. Times were tough. The economy took a big hit. It was not a good time to be in a business that relied on new construction.

Soon after, the construction company that Steve worked for closed its doors. We were both scared and confused for our future. We were carrying a hefty mortgage on our own newly constructed dream house, and now we had no income coming in.

With my son Billy only a few months old, we realized we needed to do something, and *fast*. We had a mountain of steady bills and were receiving threatening phone calls every day from various debt collectors. Steve was like a deer in the headlights, just trying to focus on finding work. As the end was near, I sat at my kitchen table, after hanging up on the last debt collector, slamming the phone with such force again and again and again, hoping the man would literally feel my thrusts, as if I reached through the phone and punched his face. In my fit of rage, I took the brown paper bag full of credit collection demands, overdue bills and statements and threw it up in the air, leaving a sea of papers on my kitchen floor. Anger and fear scorched my body, and I cried. When I opened my red, swollen eyes, now covered with black mascara running down my cheeks followed by the taste of salt in my mouth, my body slumped over surrendering to defeat, mourning the end of our dream.

Losing Your Identity

When you experience losing a job, losing a home or closing a business, it can have a devastating impact on your outlook on life. Most of us believe those things define us, that they are our identity. What happens when we believe what we have and what we do defines who we are, and then suddenly, it is all gone? We flounder; we have no idea what to do. We barely recognize who we are anymore. This type of thinking causes so many suicides.

I'm writing about this because Steve and I actually lived this nightmare but managed to get on the other side as more grounded and confident human beings. Once we brushed off our egos, we realized that we needed to *create a new normal.*

Losing a home, a business and a job all at once, was our first wake-up call as a married couple. This kind of hardship could make or break a marriage, depending on how you choose to deal with it. We could have blamed each other, bailed out and gone our separate ways. Many marriages did break up back then. However, deep down, we knew we loved each other, and were committed to making our marriage work.

Having our son Billy in our lives also gave us a new perspective. What we learned from this challenge was that it wasn't so important to have that big house or the grand job. The word *rich* took on a new meaning. We were shifting our focus, away from acquiring things, and onto the satisfaction of focusing on what matters most: family.

Living with uncertainty is scary. With uncertainty, if we stay present and open, we gain the freedom and courage to explore new things. How we deal with uncertain and unpredictable changes will forecast our future. If we stay stuck in a "bad things always happen to me" story, we'll never be able to *grow* through our challenges. If we are resilient, we rise to the occasion, finding a solution to our pain, and do whatever it takes to survive. This leads to opportunity and growth as a human being.

We were fortunate that Steve's parents offered to let us live in the apartment on the top floor of their two-family home. This enabled us to save money and rebuild our future. We were grateful to have their unconditional love and support. We were therefore able to avoid filing for bankruptcy, knowing if we did that, we would have a hard time purchasing a home in the future. This opportunity allowed us to get back on our feet, while working on paying off all of our debt.

Moving Forward After The Fall

Now, security was our top priority. In 1992, Steve found a secure job as a lineman at the local municipal light department. This was a job with benefits and a pension. While this was not Steve's dream job, it was a steady paycheck coming in. It also came with many risks, which became more frightening each day. Accidents on the job were often life threatening.

One day he was high in a bucket truck working on an outage up above. The truck started rolling down the street with no one at the wheel. Steve's coworker was supposed to stay with the truck while Steve was working on the outage. The coworker standing next to the truck turned his back while talking to the cop who was guiding traffic on the street. That is when the truck started rolling. As the truck rolled, Steve stood, frozen in horror. He then yelled down to his coworker, who quickly turned around, jumped in and got the truck's brakes on just in time.

Another time, during a "Pole Top Rescue" training exercise, a coworker tied a knot around Steve that was supposed to keep him tethered to the pole while he was climbing it. His coworker tied the knot wrong, and the rope that was holding Steve let go. He fell 30 feet off the pole, an accident that landed him in the emergency room. His body hit the ground hard. He was out of work for over six months, dealing with tendon tears, bruises and sprains.

The final serious mishap happened in a manhole explosion. Steve was underground, his pants on fire, flames everywhere. He was screaming up to the apprentice, who was supposed to be watching Steve and his other coworker in the manhole. The apprentice didn't hear him because he was talking with the cop on detail, while the rest of the work crew were running noisy equipment. Steve began to feel faint from lack of oxygen. Scared for his life, panicking that he needed to do something fast, he threw the leaking torch that caused the fire out of the manhole, the fire followed and got the crew's attention. Steve and his coworker survived.

As these frightening experiences mounted, I was more and more afraid for Steve's life. He was miserable, too. Slowly, with each day, I was witnessing his soul shriveling. Losing his spunk for life, he would come home at the end of the week, look at his paycheck, and count the years, months, and days to retirement.

I was deeply saddened. The man I married had always looked at the world as a place of endless opportunity, with excitement and enthusiasm. He was an "idea man," who thrived on taking risks and reaching higher. He would work nights and weekends. He had done whatever it took to reach his goal. Now that energy and spark were gone. The years from 1992 to 2001 were very tough ones for Steve and me.

Stay Open To Possibilities

Ten years later, in 2001, Steve was still in his municipal job. We saved enough money and bought a moderate home. One day we called a heating and air conditioning company to get a quote on installing central air in our new home.

When the young man arrived to take measurements and look over the structure of our home, I immediately thought of Steve. My mind raced as I thought, "Steve could do this job easily, with his construction background."

I tugged at Steve's sleeve. "Ask him if his company is hiring." I prodded. Steve asked the young man about job opportunities. He was happy to give Steve the owner's phone number. That night, Steve called the owner, and he agreed to meet with him to discuss possible employment options. He flew in from Philadelphia that week, and after having a lengthy conversation with Steve, hired him on the spot!

That was a risk worth taking. There could have been a thousand reasons for Steve to talk himself out of asking that question about the possibility of a job opening. Looking back at all the risks we took during the real-estate boom, and how we lost everything; we could have fearfully questioned if it could happen again. However, there was also a good chance it wouldn't. Steve and I chose to consider that a door had opened into a completely new world for us.

Fast-forward 15 years. Steve now is a partner of the Boston office of that heating and air conditioning firm, which is bringing in over $15 million dollars in revenue each year. The company has grown from five to 50+ employees. Steve himself has grown leaps and bounds in his role in the company.

It has not all been easy, though. Steve had many challenges and obstacles along the way. Each time a challenge arose, he proved to himself and others that he was *growing* through his life; he always manages to work through each challenge with focus and determination.

A good example is the morning of September 4, 2008, Steve's eighth year on the job; his crew was installing a high velocity air conditioning unit in the attic of a million-dollar home in an affluent community in Winchester, Massachusetts. It was 10:30 in the morning, and I was in my car with the radio on.

There was a breaking news story that a house caught fire in a home in Winchester, caused by workers who were installing air conditioning in the home. I froze in horror as I heard this, knowing that Steve's job was in Winchester that day. I was seconds from my home so I quickly drove back, parked, got out the car and ran into my house.

I put on the news and watched the local news stations interview Steve. My heart sank. I could see the look in his eyes. He was so distraught that something like this could happen, yet he kept himself poised and together while they asked him questions. One reporter asked, "Has this ever happened before?" Steve looked down, shook his head and said "No, never."

He explained that the holding tank the crew used to braise the line-set that attached to the condenser and air handler blew up. Gas exploded everywhere and within seconds, the house was on fire. The news showed the firefighters opening up a huge hole in the roof to access the flames. His crew was able to get themselves and the dog that was in the house out safely.

After that incident, I could not imagine how Steve was going to get through this challenge. As the days and weeks went by, he managed to face and accept the situation was just an accident. Fortunately, the owners were able to rebuild the damaged part of their house and understood that as well.

This is a prime example, that if we choose to grow, there will be more challenges along the way. These challenges test our abilities and give us more awareness of who we are.

CHAPTER 5

Surrendering To Faith

*How tragic events wake up the soul, and bring
forth unprecedented love for others and ourselves*

WHEN TRAGEDY HITS us hard, sudden illness or illness of a loved one,
we feel vulnerable and confused by the challenge of not knowing
what lies ahead. Those types of experiences force us to wake up and
pay attention to what matters most in our lives. We realize that those
things we thought were so important are not anymore.

My second son, Taylor, was born with a split mitro-valve in his
heart. I learned about his heart defect when I was just a few months
pregnant. They found it during a routine ultrasound. After my ultrasound, the doctor called me into her office.

"This baby has a serious heart condition, a split mitro-valve,
and could be fatal. You may have to decide if it makes sense
to abort, it's that serious. We will need to follow up and do
another ultrasound next week, and then we will have to make
a decision."

My head was spinning. "What did she just say? This can't be happening! What am I going to do? How could this be?" I thought.

I left the office in tears, heading home, taking the train, then a bus, while digesting all that just happened. We were living in Belmont, Massachusetts in the apartment above my in-laws at the time, the one we moved into after our real-estate crash. I walked into my apartment, saw my mother-in-law, whom I love and adore and collapsed into her arms as I told her my news and cried. All she could do was hold me, comfort me.

Steve was still working at his municipal job. When he came home from work, I told him the news. He was stunned, speechless, as he was trying to process all the information I just told him.

Steve and I went back the following week, and after doing another ultrasound, my doctor explained I should be able to go forward with the pregnancy, but they would not know the ramifications of the condition until my baby was born. Best-case scenario, it works itself out; worst-case scenario, the split valve could cause a fatal leakage, and would require immediate surgery. This news horrified both Steve and me. We had to wait until our baby was born to find answers.

The closer I got to my due date, the more nervous I felt. So, when I started having contractions, I didn't hesitate. On November 8, 1993, I went straight to Brigham and William's Hospital in Boston. It was a good thing I acted fast, because within a few hours, Taylor was born. Then, instead of holding my newborn and enjoying those precious moments after giving birth, the nurses immediately took him into ICU, where he was hooked up to machines to monitor his heart.

The waiting was excruciating. Sitting in my hospital bed, listening to the staff outside my room was torture. I was relieved when one nurse came in to say everything was looking good and that there was no leakage, and that I would be able to go to the ICU to feed my baby. I went in and held him, looking down at his beautiful face, my body exhausted from delivery, the emotional trauma, and praying everything would work out.

They released Taylor from the hospital within a few days. We had frequent visits with his pediatric cardiologist at Boston Children's Hospital, who would do a physical and administer an EKG and ultrasound to monitor the progress of Taylor's valve. The doctor then explained that if Taylor ever began turning blue, we had to get him to the hospital immediately. That was unsettling information. Steve and I got very little sleep, always having our baby by our side, checking for any signs of trouble.

When Taylor was 10 weeks old, we began to notice him having problems breathing. His breath seemed labored and he wheezed. There was a deep hollowing in his chest and stomach as he fought to breathe. I brought him to see his doctor right away. After examining Taylor, the doctor sent us home with Albuterol and a nebulizer to control his chest congestion and assist in opening up his airway. The doctor assured me this condition was unrelated to his heart, and that it was more on the lines of a bronchial cold. Within a few days, Taylor's condition worsened. His chest was heaving in and out, as he was gasping to breathe.

Frightened, I called Steve at work right away. "I'm taking Taylor in to the emergency room! He can't breathe!" I yelled.

Steve hung up and immediately headed to the hospital to meet me. When I arrived at the emergency room at Children's Hospital, nurses were waiting for us, as Taylor's doctor had called to let them know we were coming. The nurses worked swiftly to get Taylor hooked up to a nebulizer to help him breathe. Then the doctor came in and explained that Taylor had a severe case of RSV (Respiratory Syncytial Virus).

RSV is a highly contagious virus that infects the respiratory tract of most children before their second birthday. In most cases, the symptoms cause nothing more than a common cold. However, in Taylor's case, the RSV virus led to the serious problem of bronchiolitis—inflammation of the small airways of the lungs. This condition can be life threatening. His warning signs were lethargy, rapid breathing and a blue tint on his lips and fingernails. Taylor needed medical attention immediately.

RSV spreads easily by touching people or surfaces infected with the virus. Boston Children's Hospital has a specific isolation ward to treat infants with the disease. They admitted Taylor to that ward. Steve and I looked at each other then back at our baby in horror. There is no greater feeling of helplessness than watching your baby fight for his own life when there is nothing you can do.

The nurse explained that they needed to take a more proactive approach and that they were setting up an oxygen tent for Taylor. He would stay in this tent to help open up his airways. Looking at our baby confined to a domed bubble, fighting to breathe left me feeling limp and defeated. Steve and I stood outside our Taylor's new home, again praying for his life.

The nurses understood the heavy hearts of parents in such circumstances. They went out of their way to comfort Steve and me. This went on for days, and I stayed at the hospital while Steve went back and forth, needing to be home with our son, Billy, who was three years old at the time. Sleeping next to Taylor on a roll away bed, I lay listening to all the other babies hooked up to machines and oxygen. I silently shared their parents' pain and prayed their little ones would survive too.

On day 10, the doctors took Taylor out of the oxygen tent; his breathing seemed less labored, although not 100%. The nurses put him face down on their laps, and pounded his back with surprising force. They explained they needed to loosen up the phlegm in his chest to keep him breathing normally. A week later, they released Taylor from the hospital. The day we arrived home, my son Billy charged over to me with a huge smile and what felt like a mile-wide hug.

"I love you Momma!" he said.

That's when it hit me. I collapsed on the floor, broke down and cried, hugging my son Billy. I had managed to be like a rock in the hospital, needing to stay strong and available for whatever would come next. Now, all of my suppressed emotions came flooding out.

Taylor's daily routine consisted of using the nebulizer, followed by my pounding his back to loosen up any phlegm. We did this throughout his first year of his life, with frequent trips to his pediatrician, who kept a close eye on his recovery. As Taylor grew older, the chances of a recurrence would lessen as his body developed. Taylor's mitro-valve problem worked itself out, too.

Growing Through Our Challenges

As parents, we get to realize the depth of unconditional love that is within all of us. There is a hidden power that will move mountains when it comes to protecting our children. That power is useful in other aspects of our life as well. Going through this experience with my infant son brought Steve and me closer together as we found ourselves vulnerable and unable to control the outcome of this experience. We relied on each other's support and faith. We chose not to look at the bleak side, but instead, were always looking for hope. We believed in our hearts that Taylor's fate would be a good one.

That kept us moving forward. Going through this experience, on the heels of our real estate crash, brought us closer than ever.

Experiencing tragic events can be an opportunity to connect more deeply with our loved ones and ourselves. We realize the depth of love we have for one another when we fear the loss of someone we love.

Like most marriages, ours has had its share of ups and downs. I believe that there are no coincidences in this life and that every event we experience and every person we meet has intentionally been put in our path to help us grow, to get us closer to waking up to what is most important, and embracing all the challenges we face along the way.

Those Beliefs We Hold Onto That Promote Self-Sabotage

There is a total disconnect in our nation's health care today that is teaching us to hide from our feelings and emotions. When we feel sad, angry, anxious, or worry, we are told, "there's a pill for that." For years, due to the horrific time of fearing for Taylor's life and hoping that Steve survived his municipal job, I relied on mood-stabilizing medications to help me feel better about myself.

When I was in my 30's bringing up my two boys, Taylor and Billy, I was facing the pressure of working while trying to be the perfect parent and living with my own insecurities. Some days when I came home from work, I would unconsciously fall into my mother's pattern of "fight or flight" mode, screaming, yelling, and punching walls, often without even realizing it. To the outside world, I appeared to have it all together. I put on a happy face but on the inside, I was a mess. I stuffed my emotions deep inside myself hoping they would go away. My feelings and behaviors caused me to suffer chronic pain in my neck, shoulders and back. My not addressing those emotions made my physical and emotional pain worse. So, I went to the doctor to get some relief.

This was my first encounter using anti-depressants. I began taking Prozac. I soon started to experience weird side effects, including, dizziness and excessive weight gain. So, I went back to my doctor and he assured me that there were other options and we will keep trying until I found the right one. That was the beginning of my first flight of SSRI mood-stabilizing medications including Prozac, Zoloft, Wellbutrin and Paxil. In addition, because I was in so much physical pain, my doctor prescribed muscle relaxers and Valium to help relax my body and relieve my back pain. I began abusing these medications and took more than what the doctor prescribed.

At that time, Steve and I would often visit my brother David and sister-in-law Michelle's house. Our kids would play together and we always enjoyed each other's company.

One particular visit, while medicated on a heavy dose of Prozac and muscle relaxers, my sister-in-law Michelle instinctively knew something wasn't right. She asked, "Donna, what's wrong, you don't seem right?" I was so medicated; I wore a dazed look reflecting how numb I felt to feeling *any* emotion. I told her the doctor had been experimenting with various mood-stabilizers along with muscle relaxers, to help with my anxiety and back pain. The problem was, it blocked me from *all* emotion and feelings. In other words, while my new zombie-like state helped with my anxiety and numbed my pain, it also blocked me from feeling *any real* emotion.

Michelle and I had a lengthy conversation, and she offered her support and guidance about possible options to help get me to feel better. I was and still am always grateful to have her by my side. I remained on various antidepressant drugs throughout my 30s while living with numerous uncomfortable side effects. Because of my family history, I *believed* this was my fate though this approach never addressed the *root cause* of my stressors or pains. In my own life, I had downloaded my mother's unconscious behaviors of self-sabotage. At the time, my inner guidance system and I had not connected, so I just went along to get along.

CHAPTER 6

Riding Someone Else's Wave Of Success
And Knowing When It's Time To Get Off

The Physical and Emotional Effects of Disconnection –
Learning to Embrace Your True Nature

In 1997, I found a part-time data-entry position working for a law enforcement magazine. I started out working around 10 hours per week from home. As my two sons grew older and went off to school, I worked part-time in the office, doing administrative work. The owner and publisher of the magazine turned out to be one of the most influential people in my life. She became my very first mentor.

We worked really well together and she saw that my work ethic was exceptional and she appreciated that. Her never-ending drive for perfection, when it came to the magazine, the website, customer service and her relationship with others was thoroughly intriguing to me.

The goal of the magazine was to offer nationwide law enforcement officers, ranging from the beat cop all the way up to the police chief, a vehicle to share news, labor issues, human-interest stories, their victories, heartaches, and experiences on the job. The publisher was so passionate about creating this product, which stemmed from her appreciation of the law enforcement community and the sacrifices they make every day. For years, I enjoyed riding her wave of success, meeting all kinds of interesting people, while learning how to build a business from the ground up.

In 2001, I was offered a full-time position in advertising sales for both the print and online versions of the magazine—an opportunity I never would have dreamed of nor taken had it not been for my mentor. God often speaks to us through people. My mentor modeled for me the exciting nature of living on purpose, with courage, confidence and passion and having fun doing it! Her positive and courageous energy was infectious, and I gravitated towards that energy with curiosity and faith that I was there for a reason. I learned a great deal about my abilities as I challenged myself. I attended police trade shows and spoke with police chiefs and other law enforcement and military officers, as well as managers and owners of companies servicing the military and police about products such as guns, body armor, Tasers, tactical products, uniforms and much more.

As one of the largest and most well respected law enforcement magazines in the country, the magazine gained a tremendous amount of respect and popularity within the law enforcement community. Each year, during the annual "Police Chief's Conference," the magazine hosted a fundraiser supporting the families of fallen police officers.

One year, the conference took place in Los Angeles. We worked in conjunction with the Los Angeles Police Department to host an unforgettable event. When we found out that the conference was taking place in Los Angeles, the publisher decided to fly out to Los Angeles, walked onto the set of "NYPD Blue," and invited the entire cast to our fundraiser. This was a bold and courageous move. The popular TV drama, airing over a period of 12 years (1993-2005) focused on the personal and professional lives of the members of the detective's squad in the NYPD 15th Precinct. With a long list of cast members including Dennis Franz and Kim Delaney, made for an exciting night, as they mingled amongst the guests, listening to each other's stories of a day in the life of a police officer.

I was able to bring Steve with me to Los Angeles. The publisher was happy to get us rooms at The Beverly Hilton, a popular hotel that hosts many award shows such as the *Golden Globes*. While I was busy preparing for the fundraiser with the rest of our staff at the event site, Steve was back at the hotel having fun meeting all kinds of celebrities, including Robin Williams, Whoopi Goldberg and Steve Martin, who were staying at the hotel for a special roasting ceremony to honor Steve Martin.

Is This Belief Really True?

Entering the unknown is a huge risk. We don't know if we can live up to our expectations or the expectations of others. However, we'll never know our abilities if we don't try. My print media job was a path presented to me to show me that if I say "yes" instead of "no," even if it feels scary, I get to uncover more of my abilities. This erases the fear (that is just a belief we hold onto) that prohibits us from moving forward. I needed to take this step in my journey and I was grateful I did, as its purpose was to help me grow into the human being I came here to be.

My mentor helped me to have the confidence to take a job like that. With her cheering me on, I knew that I had what it took to get the job done. Without her support, I may have been happy just doing my regular office duties, in other words, playing it safe. Eventually not stretching myself would have bored me and I would have fallen into my old victim trap of blaming my unhappy circumstances on my job, boss or environment for my suffering.

All Good Things Must Come To An End

Towards the end of that ten-year period, the publisher sold the magazine and the dynamics of our congenial office started to change. My mentor stepped down from her role of running the magazine. While I respected the new CEO, who was now my boss, I found that I wanted to work fewer hours in the office, and to do more work from home.

As the dynamic of the office changed with the new ownership, I began losing interest in going to work with each passing day. And because I didn't face my emotions, I began having chronic back pain and headaches, I had outgrown my job but I just didn't know how to approach leaving it in a way that would feel comfortable for me. This was an old pattern for me that I had not yet begun to recognize.

Holding On To A Job You Outgrow Is Dangerous To Your Health

Looking back, I moved through this whole media career like a trapeze artist moves from one grip to the next; taking risks, landing and then soaring on to next one. Eventually you have to land to figure out your next step. This is where I fell short. I was unable to convey my feelings, and felt trapped, unable to make a solid choice that would enable me to make a bold move. Quit, move on and start over.

When we don't address our problems head on, be it a horrible boss, a job outgrown or disliked, a bad relationship, or an obnoxious co-worker, stress will manifest in our bodies via physical ailments such as cancer, autoimmune disorders, depression, chronic back pain, headaches, and so forth. The list is endless.

The approach I needed to take was to move on without fear. Making excuses and putting up with something that didn't resonate with me any longer would cause a chain reaction in my body, and caused me to live with chronic back, neck and shoulder pain, along with feelings of exhaustion from sleepless nights. Confronting the situation or person head on is the quickest way out of bad situation. Unfortunately, confrontation has always been my kryptonite—a lesson that kept showing up over and over in my life.

Thankfully, I finally got the courage to leave at the end of 2007.

CHAPTER 7

My Breast Cancer Diagnosis

Jolted by a sudden illness, my wake up call to life

ONE NIGHT, IN December 2005, I was sound asleep in bed when all of a sudden I woke up with my left arm moving with unmistakable force and purpose to my right breast. "Was I dreaming?" I thought. Startled, I felt around my breast, and that is when I found the lump. Only six months prior, I had had my annual mammogram, and the results had been clean.

"I can't believe this!" I thought when I felt the lump.

Steve was asleep next to me. When I woke him up to tell him what I had just found, he gave me a stunned and confused look, followed by, "You better call the doctor first thing in the morning. You don't want to take any chances." I agreed, hoping this was just a false alarm. Waiting for the morning was unbearable. As I lay there in bed, I reflected on my mother's horrible battle with breast cancer. That memory left me sweating with anxiety and apprehension. I needed to get answers fast!

My mother's breast cancer diagnosis came when she was 56 years old. Her cancer was Stage 4 and already metastasized when she discovered it. She had never had a mammogram and her doctor never proposed that she have one either. I learned this after her diagnosis and was stunned! Mom always believed cancer only happened to *other* people. She had discovered puss leaking out of one nipple, but she had written that off as just a cyst. I did not find this out until the day she told me her diagnosis. I was furious with her—and horrified at the same time.

Mom battled her cancer for five years, as it spread to other parts of her body and her bones. Her last days, to keep up with the pain, she wore a steady morphine patch and was on other heavy pain medications. Her unbreakable spirit amazed everyone who knew her. When the suffering got worse, she did not complain. At only 4'11", she had the stamina of a lion.

Witnessing my mother battle her breast cancer diagnosis taught me how important it was to persevere and not to settle or give up when hit with a physical setback, but instead to assume a warrior-like mentality and push forward, even when you are told you can't. She illustrated to me that anything is possible if you believe it. She lived a lot longer than the doctors believed she would. They all told me this. She demonstrated the power of mind over medicine. Her will to live kept her going.

That night, when I found my lump, I was 44 years old. Steve went with me to the doctor the next day. They took me right away, knowing my family history. As my doctor felt the lump, he said it felt soft like a cyst, not hard, which is characteristic of a tumor. Knowing my family history, he ordered a biopsy along with an MRI and ultrasound.

This was during the week before the Christmas holiday. Most medical facilities were half-staffed through Christmas break, which meant I would not know my results until the office reopened after January 2. That week felt like a lifetime. I went about my holiday parties, trying to have fun. I decided to let go of any anxiety; I knew if I stayed in a state of worry, it could be all for nothing.

After the holidays, I was at work when I received the call from my doctor confirming that the lump was in fact a tumor. He said I must go in to speak with him right away; we needed to discuss the game plan.

My head was spinning. Sitting in my office, I could not believe what I just heard. I felt weak, light-headed and faint. My body broke out into a sweat, as I sat at my desk with my head between my hands to catch my breath. I called Steve right away. I held onto the phone with a strong grip; one hand cuffed on the receiver so no one in the office would hear me, and told him the news. He said he would rush over to the doctor's office right away to discuss what we were going to do next.

"Everything is going to be OK, Donna, you'll beat this," he said.

Before I left work, I went in to the publisher's office and closed the door. Shaking, trying to find the strength to say aloud what just happened, I told her my news. As the blood left my face, my legs felt weak. I wore a look of disbelief and sadness and the publisher was concerned that I wouldn't be able to drive. I assured her I would be okay.

Sitting in the doctor's office, everything was coming at me so fast. He pointed out my options and told me I needed to make a decision as soon as possible. He talked about the difference between having a mastectomy or lumpectomy. Both options were viable ones. It was my decision. That was a heavy burden to bear, but having witnessed what my mother had gone through, I felt my best option was to have a mastectomy. I wanted this cancerous thing out of my body.

Because of my family history, my doctor ordered another MRI on the left breast, to rule out more cancer. To my horror, that MRI confirmed another tumor had been growing in that breast, too. This meant my surgery plan had to change; I was going to have a bi-lateral mastectomy. The prospect of that surgery was cumbersome and scary. In hindsight, I was grateful that the surgeon did not tell me everything that was going to happen. Post-surgery was unbearable, but I made it through. As I was only in my early 40's, I decided to have reconstruction. That is a personal decision and I felt for me, it was the right one.

When I followed up with the surgeon to go over my MRI and biopsy, she looked at the films and test notes, looked back at me, and her eyes opened wide in disbelief.

"Donna," she said. "I have only had one other patient with this type of tumor. You are so lucky your cancer is only at Stage One. This type of tumor grows flat, like a hand with all the fingers spreading wide, instead of in a ball, which makes it difficult to see. Usually one doesn't see or feel this type of tumor till it's too late, usually Stage Four. Miraculously your body grew a cyst on top of your tumor, which was the reason you found it so early. Someone was looking out for you." Instinctively I knew my mother had been the force that moved my hand in the middle of the night, guiding me to find my cancer.

Going through this experience was a very confusing time. I challenged myself to listen to my higher self to make a health decision, something I have never done before. With something as serious as cancer, I just wanted someone to tell me what to do. When that didn't happen, *I was forced to go within and listen to my own intuition.* As I started to listen, I knew my answer. I made my surgical choice with confidence. My doctor agreed, although he did not influence me one way or another. That was my very first personal health advocacy encounter. I took responsibility, educated myself, and came to a decision I felt was a good one.

Sudden illness will always be a challenge. There is so much information to process, and our first instinct is to shrink, because we are overwhelmed with grief and uncertainty. That is a perfectly normal reaction, and is exactly how I felt. Because the doctor left the final decision up to me, it demanded I pay attention to *me* to gain more self-awareness.

Out of that, I was able to educate myself more thoroughly on my treatment options. I even asked the surgeon for referrals to other patients who went through each of the options, so I could compare each experience. I had lengthy conversations with these kind women, and was able to make an informed decision. That was empowering.

It was torture trying to go about my everyday routine while waiting to have my surgery. I kept playing my mother's horrifying cancer experience over in my mind, and I wondered if that would be my fate. On my way to work one morning, mentally and physically exhausted from all my sleepless nights, I was in a foggy state of confusion. Then I saw a car coming down the exit ramp from the highway, heading straight towards me! I froze in horror as the agitated driver kept beeping his horn, yelling and screaming. I realized then that I was driving up the ramp going the wrong direction! I immediately turned my car around, got to the end of the exit ramp, pulled over on a side street, and sobbed, hitting the steering wheel, angry and humiliated, and feeling like a fool. Driving up the exit ramp the wrong way was a profound metaphor for how I was sleepwalking through my life. Cancer was the impetus of my awakening.

CHAPTER 8

Mind Over Medicine: Setting Your Intention To Feel Good

Self-Compassion – Intend to feel good;
redirect your thoughts in a positive way

I SAT IN my oncologist's office as she went over my chemotherapy treatment plan and explained that they were going to take an aggressive approach, due to my family history. She called it "dose-dense," which meant instead of spreading it out over a period of several months that they were going to attack it, quickly, in a period of eight weeks— one week of chemotherapy, then one week off. This approach was fast and furious, which meant very little time between treatments to feel good. When the treatments are not as closely given, you have more time to recuperate. I agreed with this option to move forward as fast as possible.

At the time, I always looked forward to my indoor cycling classes. That's why, one of the books I picked up for my post-surgery recovery was Lance Armstrong's memoir, *It's Not About the Bike: My Journey Back To Life*. (This was in early March 2006, before Armstrong's admission of using performance-enhancing drugs.) That book inspired me on many levels. It was then that I decided I was not going to play victim to this cancer thing, but instead, become a fearless warrior just as I considered Lance.

The week of my first chemotherapy treatment, I made a visit to a local bike shop in my town to purchase a bike. While the sales clerk was educating me about the features of various models, I was busy visualizing myself as the next winner of the famous Tour de France. I was going to ride my bike and conquer cancer just like Lance! The clerk said I could pick up my bike in a few days, while they fitted my shoe clamps, etc.

I showed up at my first chemotherapy session, with Stephen sitting by my side, nervous with anticipation. As the nurses were administering my chemotherapy, I was surprised how good I felt. Then the nurse explained what came next, a Prednisone drip, to help combat any nausea that may show up from my treatment. As the Prednisone drip entered my body, I was feeling optimistic, followed by feeling energized, then feeling invincible!

I looked at Stephen and said to him with an enthusiastic, wide-eyed look, as the last drop of Prednisone came out of the IV, "I'm going to pick up my new bike today!"

"What?" He said. "Donna, you're crazy, just go home and rest, you don't know how you're going to feel later on."

When we got home, Steve kept reiterating why I should just take it easy today. But, I was determined. So when he was on the phone, I snuck out of the house, and ran to the bicycle shop, which was only a fifteen minutes away, to pick up my bike.

I put on a pair of bike shoes to help improve my performance and threw my sneakers in a bag that I would tie to my bike. What I didn't consider is that although there is a good reason those bike shoes lock onto the pedals, there's also a good reason to know how to get out of them quickly. When you are riding indoors, on a stationary bike, that's never an issue.

My first ride on my new bike, as I left the store took me about 200 feet from the bike shop, where I crash landed on Massachusetts

Avenue, a busy main street in my town, my shoes still clamped in the pedals, leaving a shattered and detached mirror in my wake. As I brushed myself off, fortunately with only minor bruises, I realized I'd better put my cycling career on hold for the time being.

Emotional Impact Of Cancer

One of the most fearful and humiliating side effects of my chemotherapy treatment was hair loss. That was the very first question I asked my doctor when he was explaining my cancer protocol. "Will I lose my hair?" When I found out that I would, I was devastated. I would lie in bed at night thinking, "How on earth am I going to make it through this?" "What will I look like?" I had thick, beautiful, shoulder-length, brunette hair. I couldn't fathom how I was going to deal with losing it.

On the first day of my chemotherapy treatment, the nurses explained to me that losing my hair can be sudden or slow and that it often comes out in clumps. It could happen in the shower or I would wake up with clumps of hair on my pillow. I would have patches of bald spots before it all falls out. Visualizing this was a crushing blow to my ego. "This sucks!" I thought.

Despite my initial fears and concerns over the impact of my hair loss, I decided to take a proactive approach, bite the bullet and shave my head. I needed help and asked my hairdresser who was also a good friend to accommodate my wish. Lee was sympathetic and kind, and understood my anxiety over losing my hair. We met after hours at the salon where she worked. I walked in with a bottle of wine and my new wig. As Lee was shaving my hair, I told her all about my bike story. We both laughed and continued to drink our wine, sharing more funny stories, helping us both get through our pain. We ended the night with my trying my new wig on, while Lee styled it perfectly. I walked out of there feeling different, yet empowered. "I've got this," I thought.

Going through this experience taught me how vulnerable we can be about our appearance. I had my days when I felt ugly, looking into the mirror, pale with dark circles under my eyes, no eye lashes or brows to outline my face, and no hair. This made me realize how before cancer I focused so much on my outward beauty to establish how I felt about myself. Now, I desperately needed to find that same beauty inside.

After the bike accident, I began to experience many more sick days than good days. With each chemotherapy treatment, the nurses would send me home with a list of possible side effects. I soon realized I was experiencing close to 90 percent of them. My body felt fatigued, exhausted, and always nauseated, while suffering from severe headaches. My gums were swollen, tender and bleeding, as if I was living with years of gum disease. I grew sores inside my throat and mouth, which made it difficult to eat. I sucked on popsicles to relieve my pain and could only eat soft foods like smoothies, cool soups, yogurt and scrambled eggs. I also had sores on my hands and feet. It hurt to put on shoes, the soles of my feet were inflamed with so many sores. The doctor kept trying different medications to relieve my symptoms, but nothing helped. In a short time, I went from my usual optimistic self to feelings of despair.

Humor Is The Best Medicine

A friend of mine advised me to watch funny movies. So, I took advantage of my subscription to Netflix. It was 2006, and their video-on-demand was not yet available. They only offered DVD movie rentals that they mailed to your home. When you finished with one movie, you would return it and the next DVD would be mailed to you.

I rented as many comedies and romantic movies as I could. To my surprise, this approach helped. One of my favorite movies was *Notting Hill*. It is the story of William Thacker, a shy, lonely, divorced guy with floppy hair, played by Hugh Grant, who owns a small travel bookshop in Notting Hill, West-London. William falls in love with a Hollywood A-lister, Anna Scott, played by Julia Roberts. There was a scene when William and Anna decided to climb over a majestic wrought iron fence, to view a beautiful botanical garden on the other side. William awkwardly attempts to climb over the fence, but keeps falling. Each time he falls, he unconsciously says "Whoopsidaisies." All the while, Anna is laughing hysterically then asks,

"What did you say?"

He says "nothing."

"I don't think so!" says Anna. "You said "Whoopsidaisies! No one has said "Whoopsidaisies" for fifty years, and even then it was only little girls with blonde ringlets."

That had me laughing so hard, I had tears coming down my face. A movie that inspires one to *feel good* can be so uplifting and as I immersed myself in laughter and positive emotion, I found that I could redirect my thoughts and feelings from fear and dismay towards a more joyful and hopeful place. I still felt sick, but my moods became brighter, and as I was at the halfway point of my treatments, able to see the light at the end of the tunnel.

I realized that I needed to surrender to how my body was reacting to my treatments. I was resisting it and judging myself, as if something was wrong with me. It was difficult to accept that, with my illness, my purpose now was to rest. Because of this resistance, I was always feeling guilty. To slow down and take care of ourselves is the best medicine (aside from some strong doses of humor) we can give ourselves. We're forced to nurture ourselves, and listen to what our body needs, without feeling guilty. For the first time, I was on the receiving end, letting others help me, cook for me, shop for me, and I felt grateful to have the help.

Seven years later, in 2013, when I watched Lance's admission of using performance-enhancing drugs and bullying people who dared to tell the truth, I got an acute, queasy feeling in my stomach, followed by a deep sadness. It soon occurred to me that I was taking Lance's story much too personally. However, his successes and triumphs had served a purpose. They had motivated me. Instead of lying down in the face of my disease, I had become a courageous warrior who fought to live.

My bike ride also makes a great story as I look back at my cancer experience. Instead of focusing on and reliving all of my sick days, I pause, reflect and laugh at my bike story. That helps me find the humor in all the madness.

CHAPTER 9

Going On A High Speed Chase To Find Myself

Early in December 2008, two year's post cancer, I began my quest to find the same passion and enthusiasm that my mentor stimulated in me during my career at the magazine. I wanted to find my purpose and to have a career that was meaningful, one that I could jump into with passion. I just didn't know what that was.

During my high-speed quest to find myself, I chased after a professional title that I could claim as my own. I believed finding my life purpose meant having a tangible title like dancer, singer, doctor, lawyer, etc. next to my name. With each new job I tried, I started out eager and excited. Unfortunately, it only took a short while for me to discover I was moving in a wrong direction.

When I finally slowed down, got quiet and stopped looking *outside* of myself, I went *within*. That is when I realized my purpose was to be wholeheartedly me, without self-judgment. I began to realize my perceived weaknesses were actually my strengths, and that my uniqueness set me apart from everyone else.

Being on this high-speed chase was exhausting and humiliating. Once a month, I would walk into my local woman's networking group meeting, looking really poised and self-assured. I learned to play the "self-confidence" card really well. The term "fake it till you make it" remained stuffed tightly in my back pocket.

I did really well mingling with others in the group, but towards the end of that five-year period, in 2012, my confidence began to unravel. I was in my sixth job, working for a local health and wellness magazine, doing advertising sales. I walked into the meeting, prepared to answer the infamous question, "What are you doing... *now?*" Then Jane, the group organizer, walked over to me. As I reached out to shake her hand, I was terrified I would reveal myself by my sweaty palms.

"Hi Donna, so what are you up to, now?" Jane asked.

Even though I practiced my "elevator speech" many times in my mind, somehow it didn't come out as smooth as I hoped. In hindsight, the transparency of my anxiety was comical. As I explained my new venture, stuttering and talking in circles, Jane's eyes followed my words, as she moved her head around, then back and forth, to follow my pathetic attempt to make sense. Then she gave me "the look" I read as pity. The pain inside me was unbearable. I thought to myself, "Why on earth am I here? I hate these meetings! Why do I keep showing up and torturing myself?"

Learning To Question The Story I Was Telling Myself

That look of pity I read on Jane's face was the story I kept running in my mind. We never really know what someone else is thinking. One could look at my life and wish they had the same courage to try different things as I did. Most people would not venture down those roads of uncertainty. It was not until I looked at my life as an observer that I could acknowledge that I really was courageous. I just could not see it because I was too busy focusing on everyone else.

The Car Crash That Woke Me Up

I will always remember the day of December 22, 2012. It was at the end of my five-year period of searching for my purpose. I was driving home from an appointment, when a car came out of nowhere, heading straight towards me. I knew I needed to prepare myself for the collision as I saw the female driver was not looking at the road. As the SUV got closer, my hands gripped the steering wheel with force and I braced for impact. Her SUV struck me head on. My whole body jolted back and forth, as I slammed on my brake, and came to a complete stop upon impact. My seat belt dug into my body as I looked around to see if I was all right. The people on the street came running over to check if I was ok, I looked up, my whole body shaking, and nodded my head to indicate "yes," feeling too weak to speak aloud.

I suffered from muscular tension in my neck, shoulders and back, along with cervical disc herniation and severe whiplash from the crash. The weeks and months following the accident caused me to have no choice but to slow down, rest, and take care of my body. Now, my days were filled with therapy sessions, including acupuncture, chiropractic and massage, and plenty of rest. I was taking care of me, healing my body *and* my mind. I left my advertising sales job so that I could recover. As my life slowed down, I realized my high-speed chase to find my purpose in life was finally over.

Our Greatest Challenges Help Us Realize Our Truth

I was in a situation in which I chose to remain on autopilot. As a result, I felt powerless to change direction, trapped, with no way out. My focus was only on what was wrong, instead of considering what was right in my life. Unfortunately, it took a car crash to get my attention. Most of the pain in our lives comes from the stories we tell ourselves. We are afraid of facing the reality of a situation and accepting it for what it is.

I had the accident when I was losing control of my life. As I quieted my mind, I became present; my purpose was to heal. As I did, I learned to listen to my inner guidance, my intuition. I began to realize I was getting this purpose thing all wrong. *I was chasing something outside of myself to find my answer, instead of looking within.* This was my light bulb moment.

CHAPTER 10

The Gift Of Cancer

Sudden illness can be our launching pad for a new way of living. Opening our minds to more meaningful experiences, and living authentically, instead of by default

WHEN I WAS knee deep dealing with my cancer diagnosis, I was humbled by the heartfelt generosity of friends, family members, neighbors, kids and parents that I barely knew, who reached out to me with unique offerings of meals, help with errands, or getting my kids to their sports practices and games. Cards and letters of support came pouring in from people letting me know they were there for me.

In my print media job, my boss would call every day to reassure me that she was taking care of all of my accounts. This meant a lot, as most of my salary was commission based, which meant if I didn't sell, I wouldn't get paid. With her generous effort, I would continue to receive my normal pay, while I was going through my treatments.

This was a memorable time in my life. For the first time, I was on the receiving end of what is within all of us: generosity and unconditional love. This felt uncomfortable and overwhelming at first, as I was not accustomed to these acts of kindness and compassion. As I began to pay more attention, my understanding grew. I saw that each kind gesture a person tendered offered *them* a gift as well.

When we reach out to others, offering our own self to someone who is hurting, it brings us ten times more joy in our own life. This act of service to others feeds our soul, bringing on a feeling of abundance, instead of scarcity. We appreciate that we have more within our own life.

These acts of kindness allowed me to acknowledge that I have more than I need to be happy, and that I was going to extend myself in the same way for others. I learned first-hand that even the smallest gesture can make a huge difference in someone's life, in someone's day. Paying attention to and acting on that, was my gift to myself. I woke up and saw others through a compassionate lens.

Cancer forced me to slow down and breathe. This was my first big *shift* in life. Instead of always living my life by default, missing all the gifts that were all around me, I began to notice everything and every person I met. I expanded my sense of self-awareness, which gave birth to my finding other like-minded friends, who supported my vision of living an authentic life. People who understand that we all have struggles, and caring and validating one another while going through life's rough patches offers hope and strength to all of us.

Cancer also unleashed a burning desire for me to understand what my purpose in life was. When I was on my high-speed chase through my life, taking on six jobs in five years, busy getting licenses and certifications, I didn't realize I was in the middle of another growth period. I learned that instead of feeling as if I had failed at each job, I could see that those opportunities had *failed me*. They had failed to fulfill my passion and desire for living a more authentic life.

My Personal Shift
My personal shift started in 2009 when, in a bookstore I saw this little book with a butterfly on the cover, titled *Shift Happens!* By

Robert Holden. Intrigued, I opened the book to the introduction and read. *"Some people go through life, some people grow through life."* That phrase hit me hard. I realized at that moment, I had been *going* through my life instead of *growing* through my life.

I began picking up every book I could find on spirituality and positive thinking. I learned at lightning speed, and became fascinated by the power of our thoughts. I started to understand that most of my fears were just beliefs I held on to, some inherited from my childhood. My suffering was self-inflicted, as I struggled with all my might to "fit in," to be like everyone else. When our emotions get involved, we can't think straight and only react to our challenges. We go through our life as the passenger instead of the driver. My newfound spiritual studies helped me realize that I needed to step back and look at my situation objectively to realize what was causing me to keep chasing after something that wasn't there.

By ignoring my feelings and emotions, I was stuck in playback mode, my negative assumptions of seeing others better than me, became a self-fulfilling prophecy, and I kept creating the results I thought I deserved. I began to understand that my perception of life was the root cause of my stressors. Now the lens I looked through changed. I realized that I needed to learn to get out of my own way, in order to grow and evolve in a more positive, self-empowered way.

Finding My Strengths

Now my mind was opening up to receive new information and attitudes. I felt reborn. I suddenly was able to see my life differently and saw that I had control over my thoughts, and could change them at any given moment.

The one common thread I experienced with all of the different occupations I tried was that with each one, I would visualize myself doing them, and doing them really well. I was using the power of visualization without even realizing it. Visualizing myself in each role gave me the courage to move forward. I never second-guessed my decision to try something new when I lived this way. I also knew I was on the right path because of the way I was feeling. With each job experience, I was excited and enthusiastic, and wanted to learn as much as I could about my new venture.

That was my motivation. I could progress only if a belief resonated with me. If not, even if it was the right thing to do, or if I thought, "This is what others think I should do," I was unable to move forward with it as that would be too heavy a burden to bear, and would eventually burn me out. With each experience, I discovered more about my talents and abilities. That was my reward.

I decided to take The Myers-Briggs (MBTI) Personality Test. Katharine Cook Briggs was a voracious reader of the new psychology books coming out in Europe, and she shared her fascination with Carl Jung's latest work — in which he developed the concepts of introversion and extroversion — with her daughter, Isabel Myers. They would later use Jung's work as a basis for their own theory, which would become the Myers-Briggs Type Indicator. MBTI is their framework for classifying personality types along four distinct axes: introversion vs. extroversion, sensing vs. intuition, thinking vs. feeling and judging vs. perceiving. A person, according to their hypothesis, has one dominant preference* (The Washington Post)

Organizations around the world employ this tool to improve employee engagement and teamwork. Teachers offer it to students looking to understand more about their preferences, strengths and interests. Adults looking for a career change also use it to help them determine a direction, as I did.

Upon completing my test, I learned that my personality type was an ENFP. This stands for E, extrovert, N, intuitive, F, feelings and P, perceptive. The description of my ENFP personality type indicated that I am warmly enthusiastic and imaginative and that I enjoy trying new things, seeing life full of possibilities, and like making new connections. ENFPs enjoy working with people, which can translate into a profession in sales, teaching or in a mentoring role. ENFP's love starting up new projects and can bring a zest to them, with lots of energy, enthusiasm and creative ideas. They have an incredible ability to bring out the strengths of others, and possess a strong sense of values when it comes to decision-making, using intuition over logic. They prefer spontaneity to structure and routine.

I felt confident now to release the need to conform to what I thought I *should* be and ready to embrace myself for who I am. Now when others ask what I am doing, I can say with confidence whatever it is at that particular time. I am not afraid to try new things in fact, I thrive on them. I realize now that I get bored quickly in a more constricted atmosphere, and could never be happy working in that kind of environment. How liberating that was for me when I came to that realization.

The message that our society sends, especially to our children is, "Be perfect; don't make mistakes, or you'll look weak and incompetent." This is dangerous. In reality, making mistakes are the quickest way to learn what it is we *don't* want in order to get clear on what we *do* want.

There is always a lesson in every experience. It's important to become conscious of everything you're learning along the way. Having faith takes a lot of self-respect, and with self-respect, you gain confidence in your choices, and do not rely on others to make them for you. A great book by Terry Cole-Whittaker, *What You Think of Me is None of My Business*, talks about just this. Whittaker writes, "*Being in resistance to the flow of your natural self is Hell. Being in the flow of the spiritual life is Heaven.*"

That spiritual life of being in Heaven is the place I inhabit when I connect to my true source, spirit and soul. It is that feeling of getting goose bumps about an idea, or feeling exceptionally happy about something I want to pursue. I will not fall into the trap of overthinking and talking myself out of it, or letting others talk me out of it. There's a reason that idea popped into my mind, and I want to explore it. The more I do, the more I know that I am on the right path.

Things just started showing up in my life that directed me like a GPS does my car. The same holds true if I go the opposite direction. If I focus my attention on what makes me feel bad, like I did in the past, I would have just continued having that same negative experience.

How Did I Remove The Fear In Order To Try New Things?

I used to say to myself, "No matter how hard I try, I just can't take the next step." Or, "I can't make up my mind. Do I stay at my present job, or go after this new opportunity that looks interesting?" When I removed the "right or wrong" option out of the decision-making process, I felt much more confident in my choice. No matter what path I chose, it took me to a different destination on my journey.

A wonderful book by the late Susan Jeffers, *Feel the Fear and Do It Anyway*, talks about this in detail. Jeffers talks about when you change the way you look at your life, *both* options will be the right one. You leave behind all the fear and guilt. Jeffers writes, *"Each path is strewn with opportunities – despite the outcome."* Remove the fear, and do it anyway, allows you to realize either way, you cannot lose. What a great lesson to take from that book!

PART TWO

Growing Through Challenge

CHAPTER 11

Trusting My Body's Wisdom

Knowledge is power when it comes to our health.
Learn not to settle; investigate all your options
and alternative treatment therapies

TWO YEARS AFTER my cancer treatments, my doctor wanted to perform a bone density test on me. He explained that cancer patients could experience osteoporosis resulting from accelerated loss of bone mineral density caused by their treatment. My test showed borderline osteoporosis, so my doctor then recommended Fosamax, a medication designed to help menopausal women stop the progress of bone loss.

I was 46 years old and had loads of energy. Physical exercise was my top priority. I worked out twice a week with a personal trainer at a gym, along with doing two to three indoor cycling classes, long walks with my dog, and hours on various cardio machines.

About three months into taking Fosamax, I began to notice gradual, odd changes in my body. The joints in my hands hurt so much it was difficult for me to hold a pen to write. When I drove my car, my hands throbbed painfully while holding the steering wheel. Then my hips started aching; it was very intense when I got into or out of my car. Soon I started to feel pain and numbness simultaneously in my feet that would accelerate up my legs. It felt as if I was standing in icy water.

I stopped all my workouts. Scared and anxious, I thought this could be cancer returning, this time attacking my bones. My on-cologist ordered lab work and a CT scan. I was relieved when all the tests came back negative.

As I relaxed a little, my mind became clearer, and I remembered that my pain started right after I began taking the new drug to combat osteoporosis. I mentioned this to my primary care doctor. He told me to stop taking the Fosamax, just to be safe, although he didn't think my symptoms were related to that drug; however, I felt my symptoms might have some connection to taking this drug. That was my intuition trying to get my attention, so I decided to do a little research. I learned that a serious side effect of Fosamax was severe joint and muscle pain.

My physician referred me to a Rheumatologist at Massachusetts General Hospital. I told the Rheumatologist what I learned about the side effects of the drug I was taking. He just dismissed it as being irrelevant. He felt I had all the signs of suffering from Rheumatoid Arthritis (RA), and ordered a series of tests to confirm that diagno-sis. After the test came back positive, he explained that I would most likely have to live with this condition, and that taking medication would ease the symptoms to a tolerable level.

Hearing this diagnosis left me furious and confused. "How could this be?" I wondered. "A month ago I had lots of energy, and was working out every day. Now, I can't even do a simple walk around the block with my dog without pain?"

Overwhelmed and distraught, and realizing my healthy body was losing its vitality, left me feeling distressed and helpless—downright powerless, actually.

*"Never affirm or repeat about your health
what you do not wish to be true."*

--Ralph Waldo Trine

I Would Not Accept Wearing An RA Label On My Back

As I contemplated this latest diagnosis, I kept getting a strong feeling not to *accept* my new fate. I did what the doctor prescribed and my new RA medicine did help ease the pain somewhat, but I did not regain the level of energy and stamina I had enjoyed before I started taking Fosamax. I reported to my Rheumatologist every 3-4 weeks, while living with sporadic pain, although now it was somewhat contained by the RA medication. By this time, I had stopped taking Fosamax, and all the while, the same message kept popping into my mind, "This all started after you began taking the Fosamax."

This is when I decided to listen to my inner guidance, and not just settle into my RA diagnosis without investigating my health challenge further. One of the biggest mistakes we can make when it comes to our health is not listening to our bodies, our own intuition. When something doesn't feel right, learn to pay attention and question what's wrong. Most of the time, our logical mind will come up with all sorts of excuses not to trust our vibes, and we dismiss our intuitive feelings as being silly.

Your doctor's job is to uncover the reason for your discomfort, and offer you a diagnosis, in order to take appropriate steps and treat your *symptoms*. Usually it is with medication. This is what most of us are accustomed to, and believe to be our only option. This approach only masks your symptoms, rather than getting to the *root* cause. By uncovering the *root cause*, we can help reverse the disease and heal.

I refused to wear that RA label on my back. Such acquiescence would prevent me from seeking alternative treatments. If I just settled into that identity, my beliefs, doubts and fears would produce symptoms that are more unpleasant and I would never find a way to heal.

I chose to take a more proactive approach, and questioned if there was anything further I could do—*outside* of the Western medical model. Our body's natural state is to be healthy. Living with chronic stress and bad food choices can undermine our health and lead to disease. The design of our bodies works perfectly, if given the proper food and mindful lifestyle choices. We do not have to live with chronic inflammation and pain. Excess sugar, processed foods rife with chemicals, gluten, dairy and hormone-ridden meat, can deplete the body of vital nutrients needed for optimal health. When we eat that way, our body needs to work in overdrive, as our digestive tract processes foods that have been *chemically* processed and made solely from refined ingredients and artificial substances, which leads to chronic inflammation, damaging our healthy tissue.

Inflammation is an immune system response that tells us that something within our body is malfunctioning. Chronic inflammation is telling us that our lifestyle choices—the foods we eat, the medications we take, working long hours or sleeping too little—are destroying our bodies. Some of the symptoms of chronic inflammation will look like this:

- Ongoing joint and muscle pain
- Skin problems or red, bloodshot eyes
- Chronic allergies or asthma
- High blood pressure or blood sugar problems
- Constant fatigue or lethargy

Chronic inflammation is present when a disorder associated with it shows up, like heart disease, cancer or autoimmune diseases such as MS, Crohn's Disease or Rheumatoid Arthritis.

I diligently researched and learned as much as I could on this subject since I knew very little about nutrition or alternative medicine. This led me to Ellen, a Reiki practitioner, who offered a wealth of knowledge on both. As I told Ellen my story, she looked me in the eye and said, "Honey, stop eating wheat, gluten and dairy."

She explained how these foods could wreak havoc on your body, causing an acute inflammatory response. She then suggested I visit The D'Adamo Institute, in Portsmouth, New Hampshire, which was about an hour away from where I live.

*Dr. James D'Adamo was a renowned naturopathic for more than half a century. He passed away in 2013, but his legacy and Institute live on. He trained in the United States, Germany and Switzerland and practiced in New York, New Hampshire, Toronto, Montreal and Europe. Known as the "grandfather" of naturopathy and a pioneer in the profession, he was instrumental in establishing guidelines for licensing naturopathic practitioners in the U.S.

His first book, *One Man's Food is Someone Else's Poison*, detailed his unique, individualized diet and exercise treatment methods based on a person's blood type and RH factors. His second book, *The D'Adamo Diet*, outlined individualized needs for good health as determined by blood types, and the relevance of diet, exercise and even personality traits.*(www.dadamoinstitute.com)

Naturopathic medicine uses the theory that the human body has an innate healing ability. Naturopathic doctors (NDs) are trained to help patients enhance their bodies' ability to ward off and combat disease by using diet, exercise, lifestyle changes and cutting-edge natural therapies (www.Naturopathic.org.).

Now, I was on my way to healing myself. I met with Dr. D'Adamo and found out my blood type, which is type B. Dr. D'Adamo placed me on a strict diet, along with supplements. I mostly ate dark leafy greens and most vegetables, (I stayed away from nightshade vegetables, potatoes, peppers, tomatoes and eggplant. Nightshades are commonly associated with arthritis and joint pain), and ate lean protein and fish, fiber and protein shakes, and drank lots of water.

After examining me, Dr. D'Adamo told me my body was loaded with inflammation caused by a number of different factors. The leftover toxins from my cancer treatments, years of eating processed foods, gluten, cheese, dairy, and the Fosamax medication, had all triggered the detrimental immune responses that had been just waiting to happen. Another important ingredient that played a significant role in my inflammation stew was stress and sleepless nights.

I began a protocol of various cleansing therapies, which included colon-cleansing, sauna, and acupuncture to help release built up toxins in my body. At my doctors urging, I began a regimen of supplements to support my immune function and restore my body back to health. These treatments became my prime focus and required that I slow my life down, and demanded I pay attention to how I was taking care of myself, which gave birth to my desire to be mindful of my lifestyle choices to live a healthy life.

Be Open To Change

Prevention is the basis of Naturopathic medicine, an opposite approach from our traditional Western medicine methods. It's about becoming mindful and aware of what we are placing in our body. It's empowering us to take back control of our health, and understand that when symptoms arise, we should step back and evaluate what we've been eating and doing.

One of the most profound things I learned from this experience is that whenever I am experiencing aches and pains, or feel like my energy is low; I need to assess what I might be doing wrong. Am I getting enough sleep? How is my stress level? Am I being mindful of the foods I eat?

Most of the time I live by the 80/20 rule when it comes to food; eighty percent of the time I eat whole foods, organic fruits and vegetables and high quality meats and fish. The twenty percent is when I may have an occasional slice of pizza on the weekends, or when dining out, a few fried calamari. Those are my small indulgences that I don't want to give up, and I don't have to. I have complete control and awareness throughout the rest of the week, eating mostly fruits, vegetables, and eggs, high quality fats like avocado, coconut oil, olive oil, almonds, and organic meats, turkey, chicken, beef and fish.

I check all food labels to find out how much sugar is in every product. Sugar feeds cancer cells. I learned that four grams of sugar you see on a label is equal to one teaspoon. This is a good illustration of the simple sugar composition of most beverages and foods and it is easy to visualize. For example, a glass of orange juice may sound like a healthy option. Using this example of 33 grams per 12 oz. serving you can easily get the number of teaspoons contained in one serving by (33 divided 4). That's 8 ¼ teaspoons in one serving! Yikes! We're talking about added sugar, not sugar from naturally derived foods such as fruit. According to the American Heart Association (AHA), *the average American consumes around 22.2 teaspoons of added sugar every day. An adult women's recommended sugar intake is 5 teaspoons (20 grams) per day, adult men's recommended sugar intake is 9 teaspoons (36 grams), and children's recommended sugar intake is 3 teaspoons (12 grams). To put that in perspective, a can of soda alone can have as many as 40 grams, or about 10 teaspoons of sugar.*

To prevent eating excess sugar, I gave up all processed foods, salad dressings, fruit juice, cereal, and much more. I eliminated carbohydrates like rice, pasta and potatoes, and grains from my diet due to the severe joint pain, and low energy, which was my inflammatory response when I ate those foods. The natural and wonderful side effect of eating my new way was, of course, weight loss.

The following are steps that I learned to help bring me back to health:

- I started paying attention to the foods I ate. Were the foods I ate nourishing my body, or depleting it? Did the food come from a box, with a list of ingredients a mile long, some not even pronounceable? If so, the food is processed and is full of toxic ingredients. The same is true for sugar in foods. Excess sugar is not only detrimental to good health, it's highly addictive.
- When buying produce, there will be times when buying organic makes sense, and other times when it's not possible. Organic is usually more expensive, but in the long run way worth it. A great website is the Environmental Working Group, *www.ewg.org/foodnews/*. On this website is listed the "Dirty Dozen" of highest amount of pesticides on certain fruits and vegetables. Anything on this list is off limits. Alternatively, they list the "Clean 15" produce that is safe to purchase conventionally.
- When buying meats and fish, I pay attention to the quality. If purchasing ground beef or red meat, I feel it is best to look for grass fed, organic meat. I look for organic, hormone free, free-range chicken or turkey. I am aware that when a package says *"All Natural,"* it does not always mean a high quality product.

- Periodically, I do a 5, 10 or 21 day detox cleanse. There are many options available. I have worked with a qualified clinical nutritionist, who offered one-on-one support. I also use all of the information I gathered as a launching pad to healthier food lifestyle choices. Having a friend join me on this quest makes the journey much more fun.
- Working with a Naturopath, helped me gain access to holistic remedies, which helped me get to the root cause of my illness helping me to alleviate symptoms, without using medication and in some cases, reverse my symptoms altogether. To find one in your area, visit *www.Naturopathic.org.*
- One of the most important things that I did on my health journey was to implement a practice of mindful eating. Stress can cause us to be fatigued, and living our life on autopilot, we lose self-awareness of what we are placing into our bodies. It's hard work, but can begin a practice of intentionally choosing to take care of ourselves. This is when a journal of all the foods I ate was helpful. I have something to look back on and see where I may be slipping.

By the end of that summer in 2008, *I was symptom free.* By this time, I had ceased my RA medication. This experience proved to me the importance of becoming my own health advocate.

PART THREE

Harnessing Your Inner Guidance For Health And Wellbeing

CHAPTER 12

Cloudy With A Chance Of Change

*Learn to listen to your body, allowing
your inner guidance to lead the way when
confused about making health decisions*

As WE AGE, we inherently become wiser as we move through the many life lessons we have confronted along the way. We begin to shed our old fears and beliefs, and embrace life with a renewed sense of empowerment. We begin to trust what our intuition is telling us, instead of relying on others for their opinion or advice. This has been a liberating lesson that I have learned and it has helped me know that I am in the driver's seat of my life. I have the confidence to stay open and investigate the root cause(s) of my discomfort, in order to get to work on the healing process.

Back in 2011, I wrote a blog post about a friend of mine who thought she was going crazy because she was enduring brain fog and forgetfulness. She was short tempered, and cried for no apparent reason. She became a muddled, paranoid, and anxious person.

This story was actually mine, but I felt too much shame at the time to admit it. However, as I have witnessed others struggling with the discomfort and disconnection menopause triggered, I felt the need to discuss my experience with full disclosure. I got through my health challenge feeling more empowered, and I want to help others do the same.

When I was three years post cancer, and living my high-speed chase to find myself, I began to notice changes in my emotions. Everything that once was routine became a ginormous effort. When I came home from work and the kid's rooms were a mess, I would go into a fit of rage. It was so bad that one day I emptied out Taylor's closet, removing all the clothes out of his dressers, took anything I could get my hands on, and dumped them on the floor, leaving a huge mountain of stuff. I thought, "That'll teach him to leave his room a mess!" I was really acting crazy! Steve and the kids wore looks of disbelief when they came home, and saw that I had lost control. They knew better than to say anything, as they were witnessing me taking on the personality my mother had during her darkest days, when she would yell, scream, and punch walls.

At work in my home-office, it didn't take much to set me off. I would be banging my computer keyboard with enormous force caused by frustration, because my mind was foggy and confused and I felt disoriented. Living in this state, I grew more and more agitated. I had always been an effective multi-tasker, and prided myself on my ability to perform several tasks simultaneously. Now I could not connect the dots on anything. I looked down at the paperwork in front of me, and realized that trying to get a grip on my organization skills was hopeless. Nothing made sense. I wondered, "What on earth is happening?"

I decided to visit my primary care doctor, and explained how I was feeling. He referred me to a psychiatrist, who prescribed medications used to treat people with Bi-Polar Disorder. Since I was experiencing severe mood swings, I agreed to take this route, even though deep down I knew I was not Bi-Polar. But, my doctor felt these medications seemed a logical route, and was a good place to start.

As I began to take the medications, I felt many troubling side effects, such as tiredness, listlessness, blurred vision, and weight gain. The thought of remaining on these medications was frightening, so I began to do some research on my own. My intuition posed the question: "Why, at 47 years old, am I suddenly accepting a diagnosis of Bi-Polar?"

Sometimes when we don't know what to do, we'll just do what the doctor prescribes. That is what I had done in the past. However, deep down I *knew* something wasn't right. Through my research, I found stories from other woman with symptoms similar to mine, and all had a common thread. The average age range of these women was between 42 and 58 years old and they had been experiencing hormonal changes, ranging from mild to severe.

Commonly Known As Menopause

I was relieved to have a diagnosis that explained my present reality. This revelation, along with continued research, led me to learn about bio-identical hormones. I found a specialist in my area and after a thorough battery of tests; the doctor revealed that most of my necessary hormones for maintaining optimal health had vanished. He explained that when I stopped taking my cancer medication, it caused my hormones to take a drastic plummet, all at once, which gave me a sudden response. He put me on a customized hormone cream, to replace my depleted hormones. By now, I was off all of my previous medications. Within a week of using the cream, the clouds in my mind began to part, the sun shone brightly, and I was feeling my old self again!

My intention in writing this chapter is to pave a path for other women experiencing troublesome hormonal changes. There are about 35 million women in the United States alone who are going through this exact experience. Many of these women have reached menopause by age 50, or will soon after. Each of us experiences our body changes our own way, some better than others. My experience was on the severe side of the hormonal axis.

Today, my health protocol consists of regular visits with a nutritionist, acupuncturist, chiropractor, herbalist and Naturopath, which enables me to live a healthy life, without the use of medication. Regular exercise, yoga, Pilates, massage, meditation and play also contribute to maintaining a quality life. Any or all of these activities can make a real difference in your health and feeling of well-being.

So how do we know if a certain course of treatment is the right one? In my case, I chose not to live with the horrible side effects of medications, and knew I needed to slow down, get quiet and hear my inner guidance. When I did this, synchronicities started showing up, confirming I was on the right path. A friend referred me to a therapist to work through my emotional state during all of this. Sitting with my therapist, Danette, I told her all about my research, how I found my bio-identical doctor and told her his name.

She looked at me with wide eyes. "He changed my life! I had a horrible time dealing with 'the change'," she said. Danette had been to the same doctor! We spent the rest of the session talking all about how confusing it was to go through "the change" and how empowering it was to find relief, validating we were not going crazy.

It is important not to fall into the trap of busyness when it comes to our health. You may be thinking, "I'm too busy" or "There's no time in my day." Instead, we rely on the fast-track approach, the silver bullet, the magic pill. When we procrastinate on finding solutions to our pain, we send a message to ourselves that we are not worthy enough to feel good. That's when we settle. We sink into the pain and accept that as our fate. That's when we numb our feelings with addictions: food, overwork, alcohol or drugs.

There is a plethora of information available and some excellent websites on this subject. One of my favorites is that of woman's health expert, Dr. Christine Northrup, author of *The Wisdom of Menopause*. Dr. Northrup shares her expertise through best-selling books, audios, newsletters, radio and the Internet.

I felt that it was best to have a thorough discussion with my doctor, so I voiced my concerns before I proceeded on any treatment. I spoke with a doctor that I *trust*, who listened to my concerns, and offered solid treatment options. This needed to be a team effort, so I told my doctor all of the symptoms that were bothering me and how my body had changed.

I also reached out to friends and family for support. I found that sharing my feelings with people who were genuinely concerned for my well-being provided me with the quickest path to my own healing. This was especially true with those who had similar experiences. When we share our problems and concerns with someone we trust, instead of keeping them bottled up in a cloak of worry and shame, we begin to see the light at the end of our dark tunnel. Instead of feeling isolated, we see *hope* awaiting us.

PART FOUR

Growth And Self-Transformation

CHAPTER 13

Getting To Know *All* Of Me

DURING MY SELF-DISCOVERY process, I found out what it means to be vulnerable, to put myself "out there," to test the waters and see what I'm made of. I had the courage to show up, and give it my all, even if it meant failure. This was my "warrior persona" that I inherited post-cancer. In 2010, during my high-speed chase, one of the licenses I acquired was a Producer License, which allowed me to work in the insurance industry, as an agent selling individual health and life insurance products.

I took a job with Aflac, a well-known insurance company. The draw to me was having freedom and flexibility over my work schedule, and the unlimited earning potential. Having the reputation of a Fortune 500 Company supporting my efforts was a nice perk, too. While they offered a wide-range of health benefits, their Accident, Short Term Disability and Cancer benefits were the most popular and cost just a few dollars a week to maintain. The enticement to companies was that the employees paid for their own coverage, leaving the employer out of the cost equation.

On my first day on the job, my new boss introduced himself. He was young, enthusiastic and full of energy. I was eager to show him my abilities. He explained all the benefits I would be selling and gave me a lot of reading and promotional material with which to become familiar. Then he said, "Here's a call script and a spreadsheet of businesses in our area. I want you to call these businesses, read from this script, telling them why Aflac would make sense for their business. Your goal is to set an appointment, so we can both go out and present. You're expected to dial 100 calls a day."

I thought, "100 cold calls today? Is he serious?" This was a 1099, commission-based job, which meant if I didn't make a sale, I didn't get paid. It takes a good six to twelve months to get going in that work. I later learned that most agents last no more than six months, because they cannot sustain a living without a paycheck. I was fortunate to have Steve's income and his business was thriving, so the pressure was not on me in that way. With that said, the job opportunity is a solid one and the agents that manage to get through their challenges and bumps in the first year, do extremely well.

I sat at my cubicle, watching all the other agents with their heads down reading the script with the occasional "flinch" when someone hung up on them. I too, took many punches to my ego that first day. Sales are tough; cold call sales require balls. This is as vulnerable as you can get. You need a set of armor to take the nasty blows you receive on the other end of the phone.

"This is the fifth call from you people this week!" yelled a manager over the phone to me.

"Doesn't anyone track who's calling who?" Then he hung up with a vengeance.

"That's it!" I thought. "I'm done with these calls."

There were no set territories so all the agents were free to call the same company. Crazy, I know, but I was not going to keep getting my ass kicked without a fight. Knowing my ability to connect with people one-on-one through eye contact and personal conversation, I walked into my boss's office on Friday, just five days after I had started the job. I said, "Let me try this another way. I want to reach out to everyone I have done business with, restaurants I dine in, hair and nail salons, local hardware stores, etc., and introduce these benefits. "I can connect far better with people in person."

My approach would still be cold calling, but less of a sting because you're greeted with a smile, shake of the hand and a "What can I do for you?" attitude. I believed in the benefits I wanted to sell, so it was easier for me to work this way. My boss agreed to let me and I set out on the road on Monday.

Fast-forward ten months into this new job. I had earned three sales awards, and was opening up new business left and right. My idea had worked! But, what I hadn't realized was that I also had to *service* these accounts when the claims came in, which meant I would open up new business during the day, and service the claims at night, after I arrived home.

I soon saw that my workload required 12-hour days; I was getting more and more tired, agitated, and frustrated. Trying to keep up, my back pain flared up to the point that one morning I woke in tears.

"I can't move!" I cried. "I can't get out of bed; the pain is unbearable."

Steve looked me square in the eyes, and said, "Donna, you're doing it again. Every time you over schedule, over work, and you zone everything else out and work like mad, until you can't any more. Stop!" Then he said, "You don't have to put yourself through this."

He was right. I had to own this situation. *I* was the problem. Not the job, not the schedule; *I* caused my pain and suffering. I had totally disregarded my own wellbeing to prove something to myself. During my high-speed chase, this lesson kept popping up repeatedly, but I kept ignoring the signs. Finally, this time I received my lesson, and it was the last time I would allow overwork to damage my health.

We have many lessons to learn in life, and they will keep showing up until we get them. Mine involved mindlessly and needlessly working myself to a point where I would be living my life on autopi-lot, forgetting to take care of me. Fortunately, my Aflac job was the last time I would allow this lesson to show up in my life. It was my wake-up-call for me to pay attention to my tendency to default to an unconscious state of self-torture. Now, I finally got it. To change, we must first wake up and acknowledge our self-sabotaging habits.

It wasn't until I made a conscious choice to change how I was activating and responding to circumstances in my life that I became motivated to abandon my old habits of self-sabotage. Most of us go through our lives doing the same thing repeatedly, without ques-tioning our thoughts or actions. We wait for a crisis, illness, trauma, loss of a loved one, or other tragedy to question how we are feeling. Are we truly happy? Are we living the life we want? Are we listening to our true nature? This is when we realize we have been sleepwalk-ing, not paying attention to what truly means the most to us. We start to question why we *choose* to live this way. When we start to question those *beliefs* that are holding us hostage, we become aware of what is causing our pain. Awareness is staying present to what works and what is not working.

What if we could change our thinking process and our habits, deliberately, being proactive instead of reactive, to things in our lives that are not serving us, instead of waiting, as I did for things to get really bad, to the point where I couldn't move, living in pain and feeling like I was swimming upstream? I had no choice but to own up and face how I was feeling and what was causing it. The gift for me was waking up to this fact, and taking personal responsibility to change; that was what gave me a sense of empowerment.

In Joe Dispenza's book, *"Breaking the Habit of Being Yourself,"* he writes, *"We live by a set of memorized behaviors, thoughts, and emotional reactions, all running like computer programs behind the scenes of our con-scious awareness."*

To change, we need to be aware of our subconscious programming, our beliefs and habits, and develop new habits that will move us towards a life we intend to live. I would highly recommend reading these two books by Joe Dispenza: *Breaking the Habit of Being Yourself*, and *You are the Placebo*. In addition, Dispenza's website offers live and online classes with exercises, tools and useful information that will enable one to dive deep into why our brains work the way they do.

My own high-speed chase for success in my jobs helped me realize that my post-cancer state of "thinking positive" was not enough for me to make a significant, sustained change in my life. I had to work on mindfulness that is, staying with my present day reality as much as possible and not revisit my past, or play back my old stories and beliefs repeatedly.

Understanding The Power Of The Subconscious Mind

We learn most of our behaviors and attitudes early on, during the first seven years of our life. They get stored in our subconscious minds. Now I was beginning to understand why my pattern of always being in a fight-or-flight response mode, causing my back to go in spasms, my trapezoid muscles to swell up with pain, and being in a constant struggle just to keep my head up. I witnessed this exact behavior in my mother. I learned these behaviors through watching her react to circumstances in her own life.

It didn't take much for her to spin out of control, from an unexpected phone call from *her* mother, to a change in schedule at work, or us kids leaving dirty dishes in the sink. She would go into a fit of rage, yelling, screaming, throwing things, and slamming doors. Then for days afterwards, she would be in terrible pain, saying she had a "pinched nerve" in her neck. Her self-inflicted ills were brought on by her own subconscious reactions and beliefs; she just wasn't aware of it. Realizing this on my own journey was a "gift" to me, and is why I have gone to work on mindfulness. It was not until I looked at and started to change my own hurtful habits and beliefs that I gained the knowledge and awareness I needed to break that cycle of self-sabotage.

I thought about any of my unconscious habits that may be self-sabotaging. There is always an underlying reason to continue down that road. To do what I've always done, because it feels familiar; however when it breaks down my health, or my relationships, it's time to question the beliefs, thoughts and attitudes behind my actions.

One example of self-sabotaging behavior I had to acknowledge was that I was a shopaholic. When I was working in my print media job and needed an escape, I would shop. Spending money on clothes, shoes, items for house and for my kids became habitual. The minute I received my paycheck, I went out and spent it. It was a great high while I was doing it, but this pastime left me feeling numb soon after. Shopping was my medication and my way of avoiding my emotions. But, my habit might have been food, over working, over-exercising or anything that helped to mindlessly avoid negative emotions.

Neuroscience has recognized that the subconscious controls 95 percent of our lives. The other five percent we are operating from our conscious mind. According to Dr. Bruce Lipton, author of *The Biology of Belief*, *"Your subconscious beliefs are working either for you or against you. Becoming aware means accessing the behavioral programs in your subconscious mind so that you can change the underlying limiting or self-sabotaging thoughts that don't serve you."*

That is why it is critical to take on the practice of mindfulness, and create a *new* normal, to break free from our old habits. Now, when I catch myself "reacting" in my old way, tightening up, my muscles contracting, I stop, take a few deep breaths and observe what is causing those reactions. If taking a few deep breaths is not the answer, I try to remove myself from the situation, take a walk, a bath - anything that will get me to a calmer place where I can be objective.

Seeking Out Meditation Tools

I began doing yoga, which helped me practice mindfulness, as well as assisting me to become fully aware of my body. Another one of my favorite things to do is take nature walks with my dog. I ditched my iPod and treadmill at the gym, and now feel the energy of the swaying trees, listen to the harmony of birds singing, and smell the aroma of the plants and trees around me. That was my first attempt at meditation. I also try to quiet my mind and meditate for just a few minutes every morning. Anything we can do to quiet our minds and reflect will bring us more clarity and peace for the rest of the day. It clears away the noise, so we can tap into our essence and into our own deep intuition.

I'll Believe It When I Write It

There were many reasons I came to write this book. A few that really stand out include how I was able connect with and receive information from my higher self through my journaling. The other was Wayne Dyer. Always fascinated with Dr. Dyer's teachings and wisdom, I read his books and listened to his CDs all the time. He wrote more than 40 books, and I read close to 20 of them, along with listening to his audio programs, and watching his videos and public television broadcasts.

I found journaling to be a powerful meditation tool. Journaling can be profound in tapping into our creative energy and source. By source, I mean our higher self. The higher self is the unfiltered, un-inhibited by fear part of ourselves that offers us answers using our own intuition. Our higher self is non-judgmental, and can provide answers to our perceived problems.

Journaling enables us to explore anything that shows up in our life. It can be one of the most powerful, and at the same time calming, actions to help us tap into our internal wisdom. I learned this firsthand when I signed up for a class in March of 2015, called "The Artist Way." This 12-week self-discovery course, based on Julia Cameron's book *The Artist Way, A Spiritual Path to Higher Creativity*, helped me tap into the lost creative side within me. One of my class assignments was to write three pages a day, called "Morning Pages," for the duration of the course. I first thought was, "How can I do this for 12 weeks?"

I started out writing about whatever came to mind first thing in the morning, literally just doing a brain dump. On the first day I thought, "Well, at least I can get my "to do list" done this way. As the days and weeks went by, it astounded me what I discovered. In my journal, I was asking myself some very tough questions. The more I wrote, the more I would "answer" my own questions, as if the answers were coming through a higher power, helping me work through each question or dilemma. Fascinated, I decided to stay open to this channeling, and began to have synchronistic events show up. These "meaningful coincidences" started appearing at random times. One showed up as an unexpected email notification for a class for which I was searching.

Journaling will get you to write down what is working and what is not working in your life. It is the quickest way to gain clarity on things that otherwise seems confusing or hopeless. The more we write down our emotions and perceptions, the more we will see that there are answers; we just have not been quiet enough to perceive them. When we focus on our problems, we continue to see more problems. We need to change direction and think about all the good that we have our lives. Having an attitude of gratitude will bring more good things into our lives, and gives us a fresh, more positive point of view.

Journaling Magic – A Conversation With Dr. Wayne Dyer

In one example, I wrote in my journal that I should listen to Wayne Dyer's radio show again. It had been a good six months since I last tuned into his show. I was going through a tough time and I needed to get back on track. The day after I wrote that in my journal, I tuned into Hay House Radio, and Wayne's show was on the air. I dialed in, got through, and had a live conversation with Wayne on his show!

In May 2015, I went through a heartbreaking experience. Through a breeder in South Dakota, I found a one-and-a-half-year-old Cavachon, the same breed as my dog, Willy. I expected they would make great playmates.

The dog arrived by van, along with many other dogs late one night, at a CVS drugstore parking lot. My son, Billy came with me and thought that the fact that we were meeting the dogs for pick up in a parking lot was a little fishy. I was too excited to give it any thought. As soon as we got our dog, I saw that something was not right. When we pulled up at my house, he seemed confused and scared, and didn't want to move at all. Even though he was a year-and-a half, he acted as if this was the first day he arrived on planet Earth. He did not respond when we called him the name the breeder had given him. He didn't even look in our direction when we called him.

I managed to get him to the back yard, where it took Billy and me over two hours to get him into the house. He didn't understand what stairs were, or what a leash was, and still would not move unless it was to run frantically out of our reach. He was malnourished, with weak muscles, and seemed horrified when he looked around.

After a few days, I realized this dog did not know what it meant to be a dog. I later found out that the breeder kept the puppies in a cage, and his only purpose had been to breed more puppies. It dawned on me then that I had adopted a puppy mill dog. I had heard of them, but never dealt with one myself. The sadness I felt was profound. All I could do was hold him, and try to comfort him. My vet confirmed that this was an abused dog.

"Their website may look legitimate," the vet said, "but it's not. This happens all the time." Devastated, I fell to my knees in the office holding my dog, and cried.

I learned that the laws in some areas of this country are much more lenient than they are here in the Northeast. "There has to be something I can do for this dog," I thought. Knowing I wouldn't have the time or energy to put into training him, I called my dog trainer to do an evaluation. She said, "Donna, it would take an enormous amount of time, patience, and knowledge to train this dog. Was this your intention?"

"No," I said, acknowledging my need to surrender him. I realized I did not have the knowledge or experience to take on such a task. Broken-hearted, I remained steadfast and determined to find the right place for this helpless animal. After careful research, I was able to find a wonderful foster home through Poodle Rescue. They referred me to a young couple who take in abused dogs and rehabilitate them, helping the dogs to get used to other dogs, and then finding them a suitable home. I was so grateful to have their compassion and support; they understood the depth of sadness I felt, and reminded me that I was giving this dog a second chance.

Going through this experience, I was journaling like mad, and was angry and shocked that anyone could treat an animal this way. I had people tell me I should post on Facebook bad things about the breeder. I focused my energy on getting care and love for this dog. I chose to go in that direction, instead of festering in all of the evil. One person advised me to send him back since I paid $800. That comment shocked me.

The day I dropped my dog off at the foster home, I felt lighter, confident that things were going to be better for the dog.

When I called into Wayne Dyer's radio show, I told him about my dog experience. Wayne said to me, *"Donna, you did the right thing. You saved that dog's life. You also were right in focusing on getting him help, instead of going the other direction that wouldn't have helped him."*

Wayne talked about how I hadn't given up on the dog and how that pertains to people too. Just because that dog was abused and damaged, didn't mean that was his fate.

"You gave him a second chance," Wayne said. I will never forget that moment, and how much his words comforted my heart.

I rode 2 ½ hours every weekend to my lake house listening to Wayne's words of wisdom. Meeting him was on my bucket list. I saw he would be the keynote speaker at "I Can Do It, New York," to take place in November 2015. I signed up immediately. Sadly, on August 30, 2015, Wayne died, a few months before I could hear him speak live. I wasn't able to meet Wayne in person, but I will always cherish our telephone conversation.

CHAPTER 14

My Own Paradigm Shift

Paying attention to our passions, values and priorities

MY PERSONAL PARADIGM shift happened between 2011 and 2013, when I did The Passion Test™ Training Certification program with Janet and Chris Atwood, Co-Authors of *The Passion Test, The Effortless Path to Discovering Your Life Purpose*. This was a great experience for me and was a wonderful tool that helped me gain clarity on what in my life was most important. I was able to discover and align with my life's vision, my values and my passions. At that time, I wanted to write about and teach everything I was learning. Teaching as you learn helps you to learn faster; therefore, I started a blog. I led workshops and classes on creating a more meaningful life, with passion, intention and the ability to change your thoughts and beliefs towards achieving self-empowerment.

Now I was becoming more aware of simple pleasures while taking time for me, enjoying those moments without feeling guilty. I lost the perpetual urge to move at the speed of light, missing everything along the way. Simple things like carrying on a conversation with a stranger, complimenting a store clerk during an interaction or acting on that impulse to call a long lost friend became deeply enjoyable and rewarding.

In my workshops and classes, I asked people to connect to what makes them get up in the morning, what makes them tick, where their passion lies. Some of the questions I asked them to ask themselves were:

- What gets me up in the morning?
- What is the most important thing in the world to me?
- What do I love doing so much that I would do it all day, without pay?
- What do I want to achieve before I leave this world?
- When I am enjoying my life the most, what am I doing?
- How does my body feel?
- Am I taking care of my health?

Until we make a conscious effort to focus on the things in our lives that are the most important, will we not be able to make changes to reflect our real desires. I am always fascinated in my workshops when people start out saying their number one passion is to make more money. After working through the above questions, and doing The Passion Test™, most people realized that connection, time with family, having internal peace, a career with meaning, and helping others are really at the top of their list. I asked my students how much time and attention they were placing on their top passions/desires the answer was usually "very little."

If we don't pay attention to and take action on those things that are most important to us, such as having more quality time to spend with our loved ones, or scheduling more quiet time to take care of ourselves, we let life lead *us* instead of the other way around. Oftentimes, we are caught up in a story that provides us with a list of excuses of why we can't take action. These excuses are just false beliefs that that keep us stuck in limbo. These excuses appear real if we let them.

Acknowledge And Accept My Feelings; They Are There To Serve Me

It's important for me to realize when something in my life is not working, to question why I am holding onto old beliefs that prohibit me from seeing a different picture. A great example of this happened when Stephen and I remodeled our 30-year-old vacation home on Lake Winnipesaukee, New Hampshire. Over a period of two years, we hired contractors who renovated and rebuilt it so it would become the vacation home of our dreams. When the project was complete, its beauty surprised us. In the last phase, we hired a landscape architect to design a beautiful patio and outside living space.

After our project was completed, I noticed that Steve grew increasingly anxious to spend more time in our new lake house. He typically would drive up Friday late afternoon (a 2 ½-hour drive) after work and leave Sunday morning. This left him with one full day at the lake. When Sunday came, Steve was mentally preparing for work the next day, along with facing the two and a half hour drive (and sometimes more with heavy traffic) back home.

I asked Steve if he would be willing to think about doing a four-day workweek, which would give him more time to unwind and relax on weekends and enjoy our new space. At first, he met this idea with resistance, dismissing it entirely. His belief was he needed to be close to the office, in case something happened. I made a few suggestions, to help him see why it could be *beneficial* to both himself and his staff to implement this change. I showed him why it was important for him to pay attention to his feelings, which would only deepen if he dismissed them.

He thought about it and came to the realization that this was something he *had* to do in order to take care of himself. Now, with his new schedule, he has time to unwind and relax on weekends. He oversees his job duties as usual, taking advantage of having access to email, phone and internet while he's at the lake.

Setting clear intentions to live by according to what matters most to you will yield you the fastest results, the greatest benefits. You'll become aware of your choices, your actions, and whether or not they bring you closer to your goals or keep you stuck in a situation that is not serving your well-being.

Making My Vision Board

Making a vision board can be an exciting and powerful process; I began to place my attention on those things that are most important, but not yet manifested in my life. I made my first vision board after my high-speed chase. That was over eight years ago. I was amazed at the results. I am now on my second vision board, and plan to make a third one in the coming year.

Having a visual to refer to is very helpful and inspiring. I use magazines, photos I find on the Internet, and collect inspirational phrases, and my own photos that represent all the dreams and aspirations I want in my life. I keep my vision board in my office and refer to it daily. There are also digital resources. Famous author, Jack Canfield, known for his *Chicken Soup for the Soul* series of books, has a free downloadable app from his website *http://jackcanfield.com/free-vision-board-app/*. There are other useful websites too, including *https://dreamitalive.com*.

Changing My Beliefs Changed My Physical And Emotional Response

In the summer of 2014, an Internet radio company who had been following my blog asked me to host a weekly podcast on woman's issues. Wanting it to be more mindful and spiritually based, I saw this as an opportunity to talk about the strategies in my own life that enabled me to learn and grow, while helping others do the same.

I knew absolutely *nothing* about doing a podcast. I had never even listened to a podcast. Scared and excited at the same time, I asked myself, "What's the worst that could happen? Will I die?" Well, probably not, so I listened to my gut, and went for it.

We called the podcast "A Woman's Path to Consciousness" and it is now available on ITunes. I interviewed authors, speakers, singer/songwriters, students and teachers on subjects that were close to my heart. Topics ranged from nutrition, our education system, alternative medicine, health and wellness and spirituality. My son, Billy, was instrumental with the whole technology end of editing each podcast. He would take my raw audio, including all of my stumbles, my "umm's" and nervous stutters, and my perpetual use of the word "amazing!" and clean them up to have everything flow effortlessly.

I was grateful for his help; I doubt that I could have taken on this opportunity without him. He was having fun while learning a lot, too. Having no experience with the format of running a podcast, from interview technique to researching potential guests, I also decided to hire a radio coach. It was the best investment I could have made, and it helped me gain more confidence as I moved forward on this project.

From there I agreed to do a live show on another network. I was entering a new playing field by going live, not pre-recorded or edited. I would try it while continuing to do my weekly podcast. Since I was working with my coach each week, I felt confident in my abilities to handle this new project. Even though I knew there was more room to stumble and screw up, my excitement trumped my fear. It soon became clear that an hour-long live show was way more work than my ½-hour pre-recorded podcast.

Learning From Past Mistakes

About two months into this project, my body began giving me signals. I wasn't sleeping, my back was chronically achy, and I began to notice my old pattern emerging where I was heading down that road to hell again. My mood was shifting. Once enthusiastic, I was now irritable and short-tempered. The amount of work it took to keep these two shows afloat overwhelmed me. This time however, I knew *why* I was getting my symptoms. I was aware and felt empowered to change course. I accepted that it was time for me to stop, in order to take care of me.

This can be a difficult thing to do. We tend to judge ourselves harshly and hold onto our original expectations. If this had happened five years earlier, I would have called myself a failure. My feelings of guilt and shame would have trumped my need to take care of myself and I would have kept on going. It's important to listen to our body's wisdom, and know that it's OK to get out of a situation that is no longer serving us. Just because it once was a great situation, does not mean we need to stick with it or we will have to live with health ramifications like insomnia, back pain, headaches, fatigue and depression.

When we don't face our emotions, they—and the physical symptoms that represent them—only get worse. Shoving them under the rug and hoping everything will be fine doesn't work. We have no choice but to face them.

CHAPTER 15

Stretching My Boundaries Helped Me To Grow

"70% of what we learn comes from challenges,
20% from watching others
10% from traditional coursework and reading"

- RICH FELLER, PHD AUTHOR OF
CAREER TRANSITIONS IN TURBULENT TIMES

EVERY TIME WE try something new, whether or not we stick with it or not, we keep *growing*. Each challenge allows us to tap into a hidden power and helps us learn more about our abilities as a human being. Each time we challenge ourselves, we set the bar higher. I never would have believed a year before that I would be hosting two radio shows! This challenge proved that all you need is trust (and a little bit of courage) in your abilities. I also learned that hosting two shows was more work than I wanted. Honoring my energy when it came time for me to slow down was the right thing for me to do.

In author Brene Brown's groundbreaking book *Rising Strong*, her message is clear and concise and she has years of research to back it up. It penetrated deep into my soul. I feel she is speaking to the essence in all of us.

Brene's message is about having the courage to show up, be seen and take a risk, even if that means failing. Failing is our ally, not our enemy. It's what makes us realize exactly what we want and what we don't want, and allows our authentic self to come forward, and that is worth the fight.

> *"Hiding out, pretending, and armoring up against*
> *vulnerability are killing us; killing our spirits,*
> *our hopes, our potential, our creativity, our ability*
> *to lead, our love, our faith, and our joy."*

> - BRENE BROWN

I personally experienced this during my chase to find myself. With each job, I took a risk, then within a short period; I left, feeling like a failure. It wasn't until later, when my mind was clear, I realized those experiences *failed me*, they were not feeding my soul the way I intended them to, so I let them go. I learned a lot about my abilities and myself at that time, and I would not have been able to do so if I played it safe. Instead, I listened to my inner guidance nudging me to take a shot, which brought me, closer to my truth.

Finding My Truth

Growing and grieving through my life's obstacles forced me on a path of self-discovery. I was tired of feeling unworthy and unhealthy. This led to new experiences, and gave me the confidence to finally own and embrace my authentic self, the good, the bad and the ugly. I stopped relying on fitting in and realized nobody can do "me" as well as me. My mistakes, mishaps, bad judgments, risks, illnesses, losses, unconscious beliefs and my family history are what make me human. They all serve me in owning my truth.

I learned more about myself through these experiences. The compassion I feel for others is rooted not only by my experiences and hardships, but also from growing up with family members suffering with mental illness. I went from fear and confusion to love and compassion. Accepting my brother Bobby later in life and seeing the gift he gave me, opened my heart up to understand there is a deep meaning behind his disability.

Because of Bobby, I am much more compassionate of others living with mental illness or a disability. I understand the magnitude of the disruption it causes within the family life, while "trying to figure things out." At first, we come from a fearing of the unknown. We only see that they are different. If we are able to expand our awareness to find the many gifts that hide in disability, we begin to remove judgment. It wasn't until my adult years, when I paid attention to how Bobby was living life in the present moment, appreciating the simple things; I realized he was better off than *most* people.

People tend to make life too complicated. We are always swimming upstream, instead of yielding to the flow of life. Our judgments get in the way of seeing clearly. We judge ourselves; we judge our kids, our parents and our friends. We expect everyone to want what we want. When we are always in other people's business, we aren't taking care of our own.

As I began to make it a practice to quiet my mind, take care of my body, and allow time to self-nurture, as well as releasing energy-draining people and things, I learned that it is possible to live each day in a way that nourishes your body, mind and spirit.

CHAPTER 16

Learn to Say No – Setting Boundaries

*The greatest gift you can give yourself is to eliminate
all the negative energies from your life without guilt*

A WOMAN I met at a networking group called me one day for my opinion on something. Generally, I am happy to share my thoughts when asked. However, this woman kept me on the phone for more than an hour-and-a-half, in a one-sided conversation. I couldn't get a word in edgewise.

As I learned all about my caller's ongoing family drama, her health problems and other tragedies that were occurring in her life, it became clear that this phone call was really a venting session for her. Whenever I brought up ways to change her focus, or take action that could help her feel more empowered, she dismissed these recommendations with a laundry list of excuses. So why was she using my precious time? Because, I allowed her to use it!

We need to recognize people who invade our space, whether they appear as a friend, a sibling, mother, father, co-worker or acquaintance. For years, I tried to avoid conflict. I allowed people into my space without my permission. This caused me a tremendous amount anxiety and physical pain. Instead of acknowledging my true feelings, I stayed in the victim role by letting them overpower me.

A good example of how I stayed in the victim role took place around 2002, when I was at my print media job; the CEO of the company hired a friend of his to work alongside me. At first, I thought it was going to be nice having another woman with whom to talk and bounce around ideas. When Katie showed up at work, it was a pleasure to share stories. She engaged when talking with me and was genuinely interested in every aspect of my life. She was a young, very attractive single woman with one of those super-enthusiastic personalities who would jump for joy when you said anything. However, something about her seemed peculiar.

That is when I started to notice that Katie's efforts for approval and friendship by me and everyone else in the office had a hidden agenda. On the surface, she was a happy, team player; but behind the scenes, she was purposefully sabotaging my work to make herself look good.

I began to notice more and more of her shifty ways that appeared to be supportive, but in actuality, she was going behind my back, stealing my ideas, and taking credit for them. Astonishingly, I began to have nightmares of a wolf showing up at work and biting my head off. That must have been a metaphor for how I viewed the situation. I had an eerie feeling that something wasn't right. As I started to pay more attention to my feelings, I discovered that this colleague *was* taking the credit for some of my work, while looking over at me with a huge smile on her face, and telling me how great I was.

People Who Abuse, Exploit And Have No Regard for Your Well Being

In Dr. Phil's book, *Life Code*, he writes about people who are "BAITERS." The term BAITERS is an acronym for Backstabbers, Abusers, Imposters, Takers, Exploiters, Reckless. He says, "*These people are always gathering data and building a file on you. Everything they do, every interaction, is for a purpose. If someone is deliberately causing you pain or harm or putting you at risk by disregarding your well-being, that person is a BAITER."*

I was working alongside one! As the experiences with Katie escalated, I was more and more furious, but I kept silent. Chronically living this way can wreak havoc on our health. Not addressing our negative emotions, pretending they don't exist, causes a chain reaction within the body. It causes our blood pressure to rise, blood vessels to constrict, muscles to go into spasms and attacks our immune system. Over long periods, this can be very dangerous to our health.

The Effects Of Negative Emotions

In my mind, Katie was my boss's friend and there was no way to prevent her sabotaging me. This is another example of having a "victim" mentality. Instead of addressing the situation, I chose to allow it. I gave Katie my power. The ramifications for me were chronic back pain, insomnia, irritability and anxiety. I would come home, scream, and yell at my family, taking out my fear, tension and anger on them. I lost my vitality, felt fatigued and depressed, and powerless to change the situation.

As I walked into work one morning, after a long, sleepless night, I sat at my desk and all of a sudden, I couldn't move. The pain paralyzed me. The pain was so bad; I couldn't hold my head up; it felt like it weighed 100 lbs. I was suffering so much pain, both physical pain, and the pain of humiliation that I had let my situation get to this point. I knew I had to leave the office, but I was unable drive home. Katie jumped in and offered.

So here I was, in excruciating back, shoulder and neck pain brought on by my not addressing this co-worker head on, allowing her to dance around the office, sprinkling lies and deceit dust over me and my work. What did I do about it? Absolutely nothing! Now the woman who is sabotaging me is going to take me home and will look like hero!

As I lay down in the back seat of her car, I felt as if my whole world was crumbling. The following day, I received a call from the publisher to ask how I was feeling. She kept prodding me to explain how something like this could happen. She perceived that something was wrong.

She had no idea what I was about to tell her. I confided in her everything that was going on. She was shocked! Immediately after our conversation, she went directly to the CEO and explained the entire situation. They fired Katie on the spot.

This is a good illustration of why, instead of going months, sometimes years, putting up with a damaging issue, the answer is simple. Face the situation and face reality. Address it head on. This approach can be emotionally challenging in the short run, but lifesaving in the end. This teaches us resilience. We come out of the situation learning more about our ability to handle a problem instead of running from it, which leaves us powerless and often ill. I needed to learn to confront people or a situation when something didn't feel right, a lesson I have struggled with all my life and that I continue to work on.

CHAPTER 17

Tapping Into My *Inspired* Truth

When we choose to live a conscious life, we move by
our own inspiration, tapping into our higher self,
viewing our world full of opportunity instead of fear

MY INSPIRATION FOR writing this book is rooted in the daily spiritual practices I have developed throughout my journey. I am committed to living an inspired life, inspired, meaning "In Spirit." My goal is to live a life that reflects my innermost wishes and desires, a life that sees the world through love, not fear or judgment. In my early years, I witnessed a lot of darkness; including my grandmother's battle with her mental illness and my mother living with her dark side of coping with her mother's mental illness and her own deep depression and self-sabotaging habits. In addition, I also watched my favorite Aunt lose control of her life while suffering from Bipolar Disorder and finally, seeing my brother Bobby, losing his selfhood to schizophrenia.

It was fortunate that I was also able to witness the complete opposite in my father, who was full of light and always made me feel safe and loved.

My Greatest Teachers

I have grown to learn that certain people are in our path for a reason. A profound example of this is my marriage to Stephen. I now clearly see how he and I had to go through our journey together in this lifetime. I would not have been able to *grow* through my life without the love and support he has given me. Through my periods of growth, when I was flailing around, trying to find myself, and losing all self-awareness, Stephen stepped in to point out the obvious. I was not paying attention to what was *not* working in my life. I was swimming upstream, dismissing my emotions and feelings, hoping they would go away.

The opposite always came easy for Stephen. In his own life, he has experienced unimaginable obstacles, yet he always had the ability to get on the other side, with laser-focused determination, and not second-guessing his own judgment or worrying about *what other people thought*. That is empowering, and was always the complete opposite of my approach, which is why I believe he has been one of my greatest teachers.

When I was in my print-media sales job, I grew leaps and bounds from that experience. The publisher, my mentor, was a strong influence and she pushed me to heights of self-awareness I never would have known without her example. Her place on my path showed me my true potential. She demonstrated what it's like to be fully engaged in a mission that is near and dear to your heart, and live all out, full of passion and purpose.

This also works when people appear in our lives and make us feel miserable. I believe they are on our path to give us clarity on the things in our life with which we struggle. These people can show up as a spouse, a boss, a family member, or even a friend. When we allow someone in our life to overstep boundaries, make us feel bad, or cause us physical or emotional pain, this person is there to teach us to wake up to our feelings. There is a hidden message behind each of these experiences that exists to help us gain more self-awareness. These lessons keep appearing until we get their message. We need to be *aware* of our feelings and question why we feel the way we do. That is our *gift* in disguise.

As I learned this lesson, I became able to look at people who make me feel stressed, annoyed, or anxious, and view them as props, such as in a movie. Their purpose is to help me grow. This attitude gives me a more humorous strategy for uncovering why I feel the way I do. I ask myself, "What is in this situation that I'm not seeing?"

What we experience in our outer world is a reflection of what's going on in our inner world. If our inner world is confused, full of self-judgment and anxiety, we project those beliefs onto our outer world.

It took me a long time for me to realize I was the one responsible for my pain. No one gets to make me feel bad, stressed or anxious without my consent. When I finally learned this extremely difficult concept, I had the courage to change the way I processed those problems or obstacles that showed up in my life, empowering myself while also growing into a new awareness.

I realize now that my co-worker who was sabotaging my efforts gave me the opportunity to wake up, take ownership of my feelings, and speak up. That has been one of the most powerful lessons in my life and I'm grateful it showed up for me.

Practicing Kindness And Compassion, Instead Of Judgment And Contempt

I had the pleasure of attending the "I Can Do It" conference, sponsored by Hay House Radio, in New York City in November 2015. Four friends arrived the day before the conference started, and we went out to a nice restaurant around 3:00 p.m., before the evening rush.

It was a beautiful restaurant, and because of the time, it was empty when we arrived. The hostess sat us at a lovely table, and we were looking forward to having a nice late lunch while discussing the up-coming speakers we were all excited to be seeing throughout the week-end. When the waiter came to our table, he seemed distracted and we felt like we were a burden to him. When we ordered, he mixed up our meals, apologized, and then he disappeared. We couldn't find him anywhere. Sitting there with empty wine and water glasses, we were getting annoyed. We were thinking, "It's obvious he is not pleased that we're here, even though there's not another soul in the room!"

As he came back to our table to serve us, I kept watching him, and thought to myself, "What is this waiter's story?" I decided to test the theory of "showing kindness," and how that wins out over any-thing else. When he came back to our table again, I proceeded to ask him his name, where he lived, and if he had a family. We found out he just moved here from Brazil and that this waiter job was one out of the three jobs he was holding. He was married, with three kids, and worked around the clock to survive in New York. He went on to say he loves New York and all that it has to offer. He was genuinely grateful to be living here.

As we talked with the waiter, he grew more excited to share his story with us. He was so pleased he came around the table and gave us each a free glass of wine! This example demonstrated to us that we never know what is going on with another human being. If our life contains judgment, contempt or fear, then we will project that onto other people, without even realizing it. We were all pleasantly surprised at how nice this waiter really was, and realized we had been judging him and creating a story about him that was totally off base.

Practicing Self-Awareness And Self-Love
All of my physical setbacks—my RA diagnosis, my sudden severe menopausal symptoms, and my excruciating back pain—led me to

an awareness for which I am profoundly grateful. I woke up to how I was taking care of my body (or neglecting it) and how I was allowing others to dictate how I would feel. This led me to embrace and accept that practicing self-care is necessary. In the classes and workshops I have led, I have seen that this way of thinking is a huge blind spot for most women. We tend to put ourselves last and hope that "someday" we can nurture our own needs. This is probably the most detrimental outlook we hold. Who is going to take care of *our* needs if we don't? We tend to gravitate towards other women who think the same way we do, for support. We need to stop this madness!

The following section contains lessons learned in my journey that I hope will be of help to my readers. Please continue reading and think about what you read. Answer the questions that I present as they apply to your circumstances. I am formatting this section as a companion workbook, so feel free to write directly in your book. If you do not already journal, then let this exercise be the start of your journaling!

PART FIVE

Lessons Learned and Tips for My Readers

CHAPTER 18

Where Do We Start?

THE PURPOSE OF this book is to inspire you to learn and grow from the many challenges presented to you in your own journey. Life isn't meant to be perfect. Our stories are not perfect. Some of the most profound life lessons learned are from the many struggles endured during our journey including those horrific life events such as an illness, loss of a loved one, losing a job, challenging financial situation or a child dangerously succumbing to drugs and alcohol. We get to choose how we deal with each situation. Instead of hitting the "pause" button, and replaying our story repeatedly while gaining a powerful vortex-like momentum of victimhood, we hit the "delete" button, and begin a new story, one that is full of optimism, hope, courage and strength.

By staying focused on our goal, the result we desire, we choose a better way. A good example of this is in my own life, it would have made sense to stay on anti-depressants at my doctor's advice. After all, with my family history, that would be the logical path. Instead, my inner guidance kept nudging me to question what I heard. My desire to be healthy made me want to pursue another way. Intuition is our God-given gift and is one of the most powerful tools to have in your corner during difficult times. Once you start playing with it, you'll be more confident in your choices and actions, which lead to a more inspired way of living.

How Can We Face Our Future With Hope And Courage After A Major Life Event?

If you haven't done so already, start journaling. Not only will this help you get your self-sabotaging thoughts and fears down on paper, it will also offer you more information on what you are not seeing in this situation. Journaling will help you release pent up emotions that have been stuck inside you, prohibiting your creative energy from coming through. You can't allow new thoughts to enter if you don't dump the old ones. Sounds simple, and it is. Below are some questions that may help you peel away at discomfort, getting to the root of your pain.

- How long has this situation played the leading role in your life?
- Has your situation limited your ability to try new things?
- If you had a close friend going through the same situation, what would you advise her to do?
- In this situation, what have you learned about yourself that you would otherwise not know had you not gone through this experience?
- How have you contributed to your own pain? Have you allowed a situation or person to dictate the course of your life by not paying attention to your inner guidance?
- What thoughts are you holding on to that prohibit you from moving forward? Can you find a way to let them go? If you remove those thoughts, how does it feel?

Fear is the number one reason we don't move forward. The following exercise is an example of how we can turn around our fear to a more positive outcome.

EXERCISE: Using a failed relationship as an example:

You: I don't trust men. I gave my all for the last 15 years and was lied to and cheated on. There are no good ones left.

Instead, you say: I am open and receptive to love and trust. My experiences taught me exactly what I needed to learn about myself, and what I want in a relationship. I now have clarity, and I will know when the right man comes along.

You see, it's all in our inner dialog. The latter example will help you open up to new experiences and find the perfect partner who will *WOW* you! The first dialog will hold you captive, and you will always keep attracting those jerks you want to avoid in the first place! You will also understand that you needed to go through the bad partner in order to get clear on what you want in a great one!

How Do I Find The Courage To Try New Things?

We begin by acknowledging our feelings, and knowing that they are there to serve us. Even the smallest baby step in the direction of our desires helps us to release the fears that we hold. One of the beautiful things about having a revelation like this is it starts to get our creative juices flowing and we begin to notice things that weren't there before. Maybe we sign up for a class, or pick up a special book that looks interesting. We start to "lean in" to a new situation, like dipping our toe in the water to test the temperature.

Get out your journal or write directly in this book, and start making a list by asking yourself questions such as:

- Is there a volunteer opportunity I could participate in that could broaden my knowledge of a subject or field that intrigues me?
- What are my natural talents?
- What do other people say I'm good at?
- What kinds of books do I like to read?
- What activities do I enjoy?
- If I could spend my days any way I want to, how would I spend them?
- Do I like routine or is having freedom to make my own hours important?
- Do I like working outdoors or inside with a team of people who inspire me?
- Who is working in that field that I can talk to and gain useful information?

The more we do this, the more we begin to notice signs placed on our path to assist us in getting closer to our real desires. Those signs can be a stranger you talk to on the train who works for a company you have been researching. You could meet someone at a networking event, who recently left her "safe" job and started her own business. When those types of synchronistic events show up, it's important that we be aware of their potential to lead us in the new direction we want to pursue.

Seeing The Teachers In Your Life

Think about the teachers that are showing up in your life. Those people have been a huge inspiration in your own life. What you see in them is in you. You just need to tap into that internal awareness.

Those teachers that show up that can also cause us pain and can be difficult to tolerate. Maybe you have never viewed people that cause you stress, pain or anxiety that way. Know they are mirroring back to you your own fears, thoughts and beliefs. When you open your heart to find your truth, you become empowered.

- Get out your journal and start your list of people who have inspired you. What qualities in them do you admire? Can you see those qualities in yourself?
- List the people in your life who make you agitated or angry. What is in that relationship that is driving you crazy? Write away, don't hold back, and be honest.
- Now, dive deep and ask yourself what you need to do in order to stop those feelings of frustration. Remember Katie, my co-worker? I put up with her sabotaging my work, and remained quiet about it. My stress manifested painfully in my body and caused me to be out of work for over two weeks with excruciating back pain. All because I didn't speak up when I should. That was a valuable (and painful) lesson I needed to learn. My co-worker was *my greatest teacher* when it came to that lesson. Now, think about someone in your life who is causing you discomfort, then journal about why you are in this circumstance and determine if you can unravel the hidden message and move forward.

Are You With Friends That Inspire You Or Drain You?

Think about your friends and with whom you are spending your days. Look to see whom your tribe-of-influence is. Are you spending time with friends who are inspiring you to live a better life or are you among friends who are stuck in self-pity, blaming their life on everyone else or every situation that is challenging them? If the latter is true, they may feel powerless to change, and will be looking for friends who support this kind of thinking. Do you want to be one of those friends who support this victimology? Playing the victim is like offering your life on a silver platter to someone else, giving them control, as if they are a puppeteer and you are the puppet.

So, take inventory of your friends. If they are not *growing* through life, it's time to let them go. It doesn't mean you don't like or love them. You are just giving yourself permission to seek others who have the vision to be greater than what they are now. These friends will inspire you to do the same.

- Make a list of your five closest friends. What qualities in them do you admire?
- Now, make a list of those friends who are bringing you down. Can you find a way to let go, in order to grow?

Change - If Not Now, When?

During a class I taught on "Creating a Life That Matters," I noticed that the group all had a common thread. When I asked them to pick from a list of values that reflected what was important to them, the words *inner peace, integrity, freedom, fun, creativity* often came up. In order to live by these values, we need to nurture our own self, and love and embrace our own needs first. I discovered that when I questioned them, their responses contained a long list of excuses for why they were not taking care of themselves, mostly putting other people's needs first.

I kept hearing: "I need to get my kids through college first."

"My parents are elderly and need me."

"I'm waiting to retire."

These are just a few examples of the excuses.

One day, before I was about to start the class, I looked up the meaning of "Self-Love" in the *Merriam Webster's Dictionary*. Here is what I found:

a: conceit

b: regard for one's own happiness or advantage

It's no wonder we deny ourselves self-love, self-nurture, and self-respect!!! Those definitions are barbaric, and evidence of how the world thinks. This does not have to be *your* truth. I would like you to open up to new possibilities and entertain the art of saying "no" when you feel the urge, take time away to re-energize, and learn to respect the beautiful body you were given.

I have come to this awareness through the many lessons I have learned throughout my life. When circumstances and people show up and drain my energy, I have the power and awareness to stop it. Our power lies in setting clear intentions for living a life that truly resonates with our spirit, our inner guidance. That is where true power comes from. It's the difference between our ability to work through our challenges with confidence, or going in the opposite direction from our truth, which leaves us feeling and acting power-less, and drains our life force.

When I started paying attention to what is absolutely non-negotiable in my life, and began my practice of self-love and self-awareness, I asked myself questions like: What is draining my energy, and how can I change that to a more empowered state? What self-sabotaging habits do I mindlessly engage in, and how can I stop doing them? What physical activities can I participate in to help energize my body? What can I do to help me gain more clarity?

Here is a list of my always-growing non-negotiables that I have inherited from my life lessons throughout my journey.

- I will not become a victim. I will take full responsibility for everything that shows up in my life, and offers me a sense of empowerment.
- I will be an observer of each of my thoughts and question if they are a judgment or false belief, and if so, will look for a more empowering thought.
- I will fuel my body every day with nutrient dense fruits, vegetables and high quality meats and fish.
- I will practice Yoga and Pilates to help me stay focused and mindful of my intention to have a healthy body.
- I will let go of people who no longer serve me in living a life full of optimism.
- I will embrace new experiences, always challenging myself.
- I will help others either directly or indirectly through the touch of a hand, a meaningful conversation, or a simple acknowledgment of their struggles; showing compassion, not casting judgment.
- I will release the guilt when I need to say "no," understanding it is in my best interest to take care of me.
- I understand that I can only control how I feel, not how others feel, and abandon the need to change them.
- I will trust my intuition and listen to my inner guidance about what others are telling me.
- I will set a daily intention to live by my values, pay attention to my thoughts, and stay mindful of how I am feeling.

- I will find joy in simple pleasures: snuggle with my dog, walk in nature, have meaningful conversations with Stephen and friends, listen to Billy and Taylor's lives as they grow and experience their own journeys.
- I will have compassion for others without judgment, seeing they are on their path, and doing the best they can with what they have, yet not allowing toxic people into *my* space.
- I will not engage in gossip, seeing it as only a weakness, and having the awareness and integrity to walk away.
- I will take care of my body through acupuncture, massage, yoga, soothing baths, and quiet meditative moments, without feeling guilty.
- I will journal, asking my own inner guidance for help when faced with challenging decisions I need to make.
- I will spend time with my tribe-of-influence, who feed my soul.

What Are Your Non-Negotiables?

Start paying attention to what is important, and what is absolutely non-negotiable to you as you practice self-love and self-awareness! Look into a yoga retreat or a weekend spiritual workshop, even meditating on your own—anything that will open you up to mindfulness and new possibilities that will offer you a different, broader perspective. Can you set aside time to play? Creativity helps our soul and spirit thrive. We tap into an awareness that channels our true nature. We are happiest when we are creative.

Take out your journal and start your list of non-negotiables. Keep them in a place where you can reflect on them daily.

By practicing this awareness, we learn the true meaning of self-love. By mindfully taking care of ourselves, we will be available for others in a more meaningful way. In order for us to put our world in order, we must first cultivate our own lives and know where our heart lies. That's when we can begin to help others see *their* light. Living by example is the most powerful way to show others how to *grow* in their own life.

Your Paradigm Shift

You have to believe it to achieve it.
Is your self-talk empowering you or disempowering you?

What do you do when you find yourself thinking about making a career change, and you're not sure which direction to take? This longing for more meaning and purpose has been brewing inside you for some time, and because of your life circumstances, you've dismissed the notion to take action, fearing that would not be the responsible thing to do. Your inner dialog could look something like this:

"Who am I kidding? What do I know about this kind of work? No one will hire me."

Or, "I have never run a business before, how can I possibly start one at *my* age?" Though these are just stories we are telling ourselves, we believe them. This kind of thinking will paralyze our ability to see clearly and keeps us stuck and feeling powerless to change direction. Becoming aware of our thoughts is paramount.

Some of the beliefs that are holding you back could look like this:

- I'm too old to try something new.
- I don't have the knowledge or training in the field I'm interested in.
- Others know so much more than I do.
- I don't have the time to invest in myself.

- I'm too busy taking care of everyone else.
- That's being selfish; what would other people say?
- Change is too much of a risk; I feel safe where I am.
- I never follow through with anything; it's no use in trying.
- Changing at my age is dangerous, that's a fact. I see it all the time.

There are more universal beliefs I could list, but you get the picture. When we believe what we think, we will find ways to prove ourselves right. I am sure you could find someone who tried to take a risk, and failed – that is your proof there no use in trying. Or, you know more than one person who talks about getting into a different line of work, but can't because they feel they don't have the training or knowledge to take the leap. It is so important to make a paradigm shift – *away* from the unconscious and *into* being conscious - that is staying present and open to opportunity.

Learn to observe and question the limiting beliefs you might be telling yourself. It is just as easy to take the opposite approach. I know you could find someone in their 50's 60's or 70's or older who started their own business or is working in a completely different field from the one they worked in in their youth. I know of several people who have done this and are thriving. Not only are they thriving, but also they are using their wisdom, their passion and zest for life, and their talents serving others in a positive way.

Their self-talk could look like this:

- It's my time, I get to live my life for me.
- I am passionate about making a difference in other people's lives.
- I can do anything I put my mind to; I have the awareness to know what is best for me.

- I am able to tell others what I have to offer and share my whole self with the world.
- I choose to learn and grow until the day I die; living this way feeds my soul.
- My past is my past and doesn't control my future.
- I create my reality and choose my thoughts wisely.
- My life is full of opportunities and I trust everything is working out for my highest good.

Just looking over these two lists, you can see the one that gets you motivated to feel more empowered. If you choose to believe that anything is possible, then it will be true. It is helpful to engage a trusted friend, someone who is in your tribe-of-influence, a friend who aspires to more greatness in her own life.

People like this will point out your gifts and talents, and not your perceived weaknesses. Whenever I feel vulnerable and start running a well-worn fear story in my mind, I reach out to one of my close friends to gain perspective. This gives me clarity on the situation, and I always feel better. I hope it does the same for you!

If you don't take action, you let fear dictate your future, and never experience what it's like to tap into your own gifts and talents and passions. Taking a leap of faith into the unknown feels terrifying yet exhilarating simultaneously.

Self-Reflection

- What is your intuition telling you? Can you see yourself moving down the path you have chosen?
- Think about that opportunity presenting itself to you. What beliefs are you clinging to that are holding you back?

Question whether that is just fear showing up or perhaps you just need to undertake more information gathering or training before you step into the new opportunity.

- Find a trusted friend, coach, or counselor who will give you honest feedback.

Making The Shift Away From Negative Energy Towards Positive Energy

When we become aware of people and things that are not promoting our well-being, and deliberately take steps to improve the quality of our lives by eliminating those negative influences, we go from victim to victor. When we do this, we'll crave and attract more of this positive energy.

This will be the tipping point, where we begin to see the benefits of letting go of all the negative people and things that don't serve us, and start to focus on all the positive things we want to manifest.

We start attracting new people and circumstances when we focus our attention this way, bringing more energy that is positive to us. We gain new experiences to reflect our new outlook.

Take out your journal or a notebook; make a list of people or circumstances in your life that are important to you, and listen to your heart. Now, think about anyone who is draining your energy and ask yourself "Why am I accepting this into my life?" Instead of allowing a negative family member, friend or colleague to invade your personal space, don't tolerate these toxic relationships. Learn to set limits on these people. First, try to have an honest conversation to express your feelings. If that doesn't work, give yourself permission to limit contact with that person or situation. It's also important to realize that the energy that you put out will always come back to you. If you're conjuring up a story in your mind, painting a picture of how bad the encounter will be, you have already set the stage to have conflict. When you can be mindful of that when faced with a family member, colleague or friend, who pushes your buttons, it will save you a lot of inner turmoil. Try to comprehend where they are coming from. Why do they act this way? What circumstances in their life caused their beliefs? They are projecting their own truth. And, when you let their words or actions upset you, you're sending a message that you **agree** with them. If you can let it go, and know this does not have to be your truth, you release your anger, which gives you inner peace, as you focus on taking care of yourself and not letting others into your sacred space.

If we don't honor ourselves by setting clear boundaries, we remain the main character in our victim story, letting others dictate how we move through life. Learn to accept that *you* deserve to feel better, without carrying around guilt. Try to see that they are only doing the best they can, with where they are on their *own* journey. You can't change them, and why would you want to? When we're busy focusing our attention on them, we are not paying attention to our own life. Showing compassion, yet giving yourself permission to move on, will be your gift. This is the power of forgiveness. You will be able to grow and move on in an empowering, healthy way. The alternative is bottling up your worries, feelings and opinions, which stifle your well-being.

That Eerie *Sixth Sense* Is The Guidepost Towards The Truth

In setting boundaries, we must listen to our inner intuition, those messages that are trying to get through to us. Intuition helps us recognize when something isn't right. We get a funny feeling, a *sixth sense* and can usually know when someone is using his or her own agenda on our dime. Those negative emotions we feel are there for a reason. We need to be aware when these emotions show up, and not dismiss them as being silly. When we ignore our own feelings, we are putting other people's health and welfare ahead of our own.

The sad truth is this can go on for years, causing a lot of unnecessary internal blame, shame and discomfort. When we tackle the situation head on, we put the brakes on whatever exploitation train is in our lives, and stop fueling the engine that keeps it going. We need to be aware that we are responsible for making the choice between fueling or not fueling that engine.

So how do we stop people from draining our life force? We start by voicing our own concerns and opinions, acknowledging them while respecting others and ourselves. To put it into a larger perspective, ask yourself, "Would I allow someone to treat my child this way?" We are fearless warriors when it comes to our children and others we love. We should take the same action for protecting ourselves.

Learn To Say "No"

Learning to say "no" is an important step towards setting boundaries and practicing self-care. If you are feeling tired, overwhelmed, or just not in the mood…you can say "No," and release the guilt. When you feel guilty that you are letting others down, you play the victim, as if you don't have the right to change direction on your own. You deserve to feel good. You deserve to protect yourself from people and things that make you feel bad. You deserve to honor all that is inside of you.

List Your Self-Sabotaging Habits

Throughout this book, I talk about the physical and emotional pain that was brought on by my fears and limiting beliefs about myself. I needed to go to work on mindfulness and become *aware* of my default mechanisms. Once we are *aware* of how we *react* to our challenges, we can go to work on purposefully responding in a more empowered state.

- What self-sabotaging habits are you mindlessly engaged in?
- Can you start a practice of awareness, noticing when you default back towards those damaging habits?
- How can you go to work on reprogramming those habits? Talk to a friend, coach or counselor. Admitting those habits is the first step, as you begin to hold yourself accountable whenever you fall prey to sleepwalking again.
- Write down a clear intention. What does it feel like to release a damaging habit? Can you visualize your new life when you remove this habit? Maybe you'll save money by not shopping as much. Or, you gain health, by paying attention to the foods you eat. Incorporating more nutrient-dense vegetables, fruits and whole grains will fuel your body, and remove the processed foods that will deplete it.

The first step is setting a clear intention. That starts the ball rolling and brings movement towards a new course of action.

Embracing A Loved One's Disability

I talk about my older brother Bobby and how his Schizophrenic diagnosis impacted my life. I learned a great deal about myself through

Bobby's disease, and am grateful for the lessons he has taught me. If you are dealing with a loved one going through a mental, physical, or emotional disorder, can you find solace by embracing the spiritual message behind their disability?

- What have you learned about yourself by witnessing their struggle?
- What life lessons showed up for you that would otherwise not if you didn't have this experience?
- Can you find the gift that is in their disability?
- How has their disability changed you for the better?

How Have You Grown From The Losses In Your Life?

Staying resilient in tough times, means to fight an uphill battle, believing that if you stay focused and determined, you will achieve your desired result. When Steve and I had our first *wake-up-call* as a married couple, losing a house, a job and a business all at once, we knew we were going to make it to the other side, as long as we stayed focused, determined not to let our story define us. Instead, we chose to keep moving, trusting that things were going to work out. The alternative would be a long, miserable life, clinging onto our unfortunate experience like a security blanket, blocking the flow of abundance coming to us.

- Have you experienced a major loss?
- Were you able to find inspiration to create a "new normal" after this experience?
- What have you learned about yourself by going through this experience?

- List the people and things in your life today for whom you are grateful. When we can be in appreciation for the simple pleasures we have, we move our energy away from feelings of despair into a joyful existence.

Staying Curious Will Keep You Alive

"Curiosity killed the cat" is a century old proverb to warn of the dangers of unnecessary investigation or experimentation. This analogy couldn't be further from the truth when it comes to living our lives. I hope by reading this book, you find the courage to be curious about whatever lies ahead in your future.

Dreaming of a life that resonates with your soul appears very early as a small child. As children, we believe in the power of our imagination, and use it with such force that we embody anything we place our attention on and have fun while doing so. The damage starts as we grow older and we inherit other people's attitudes and beliefs. The danger to us is we carry those limiting beliefs throughout our entire adult lives, without questioning them. They remain powerful and strong because we unconsciously agree with them and believe we have no other choice.

When our beliefs, stories and habits tear away at our happiness, health and vitality, we need to recognize that we have the power to choose another way. Finding courage takes practice, just like any other goal, and you must be willing to put the time and effort it takes to gain the strength to utilize this gift. One step at a time is all it takes, and you'll be closer to your truth, and be a much happier person for it.

Adult Self Writes Letter To Child Self

This exercise will open you up to see the many gifts and lessons you have learned through the challenges you have endured in your own life. When we can reflect on our experiences through a compassionate lens, our highest self, we are able to drop the judgment. We can appreciate how much courage it took to navigate through our struggles.

In this exercise, take a moment to reflect on specific challenging times. Can you find the gift you received by going through those challenges? Now, have your adult self, write a letter to your child self, reflecting on how you grew through those challenges and how that impacted your life. What would you say to that child?

Below is a letter that I wrote to my child self. You can use this example. Feel free to elaborate as much as possible. Have fun with this. As you reflect back, you will gain clarity and remember that your life's purpose is to be wholeheartedly you.

My Dearest Donna,

I am so proud of you. Look back to when you were a young girl, afraid, confused and keeping silent. The odds were against you, all of the darkness, sadness and grief. You struggled with your identity as a young girl, never feeling like you were smart or worthy enough.

But you persevered through the madness, stumbled a lot along the way, and grew through all of your obstacles. You opened your heart up choosing love over fear. That is the real you. You can achieve anything you want as long as you remember that. Your purpose is to shine that light onto others and demonstrate how important it is to be authentically whole and honest. Don't stop being curious. Don't stop learning. Don't stop loving.

Love,

Donna

Appendix A

THE FOLLOWING BOOKS and websites have been instrumental to my healing journey to wellness.

1. *Wheat Belly*, by William Davis. The author looks at how eliminating wheat, even those so called "healthy grains," from our diet can lead to permanent weight loss, as well as relief from a wide range of health and digestive problems. When I gave up wheat, I saw a dramatic decrease in my RA pain.
2. *FMTV.com* (Food Matters TV) is loaded with topics on health and wellness, full of inspirational health & wellness documentaries, extended interviews with leading health experts, fun and healthy recipe videos, and yoga, exercise and meditation programs.
3. *The Blood Sugar Solution 10-Day Detox Diet*, by Mark Hyman, M.D.

   Dr. Hyman offers practical solutions to help you break your food addictions
4. *Meals that Heal Inflammation*, by Julie Dalinuk,

   Dalinuk provides the tools you need to transition towards healthy eating and get to the root of your illness. She helps you learn how to reverse inflammation naturally.
5. *Mind over Medicine*, by Lissa Rankin, M.D.

A physician, speaker, founder of the Whole Health Medicine Institute, and spiritual seeker, Dr. Rankin is passionate about what makes people optimally healthy and what predisposes them to illness. As she became aware of how fear dominates modern culture and how such fear predisposes us not only to unhappiness but also to disease, she began researching ways to befriend fear so we can let it heal and liberate us, opening us up to greater compassion, not just for others, but for ourselves.

6. Kimberly Snyder, C.N., Author of *The Beauty Detox Foods*, and *The Beauty Detox Solution* has developed a whole foods approach to gorgeous skin, as well as to rid your body of toxins so you can look and feel your best.

7. To learn more about bio-identical hormone therapy, visit www.bodylogicmd.com.

8. *The Right Questions*, by Debbie Ford

   The late Debbie Ford, offers ten profound questions that will change your approach to making choices. This quick and easy read, will have you question your present-day reality and offers a clear understanding and awareness of why we do what we do, and provides tools to help you create the life you always wanted.

9. *The Passion Test*, Janet Bray Attwood and Chris Attwood

   The Effortless Path to Discovering Your Life Purpose – I have personally trained with Janet and Chris Attwood. This is an outstanding book and tool. This book will help you create a life that truly resonates with your soul, to live your life according to what matters most.

10. *The Success Principles*, Jack Canfield

    How to Get from Where You Are to Where You Want to Be – This book offers so many thought-provoking insights, memorable stories and exercises that will transform the way you live. You'll learn to increase your confidence to make the choice, and learn to take 100% of responsibility for everything that shows up for you.

11. *The Power of Intention, Dr. Wayne Dyer*

Learn to Co-Create Your World Your way – As Dr. Dyer writes *"Intention is a force in the universe, and everything and everyone is connected to this invisible force."* Dr. Dyer spent years researching intention as a force in the universe, and how that allows humans to co-create their life using this force. He demonstrates the importance of paying attention to our thoughts, feelings and actions.

12. *The Art of Extreme Self Care*, Cheryl Richardson

Cheryl offers 12 strategies to transform your life one month at a time. This book contains many personal stories of Cheryl and others. It illustrates how practicing self-care becomes a way of life.

13. *Rising Strong*, Brené Brown, PhD. LMSW

Brené says… "If we are brave enough, often enough, we will fall. This is a book about what it takes to get back up." This is a powerful read, and remains a staple on my bookshelf. Backed by years of research, the author uses her own personal stories and struggles, which force us to look at our own stories, embracing them for what they are, to find and own our truth.

About the Author

DONNA IS THE founder of Finding Your Health and is a Certified Holistic Health Coach who empowers individuals to make positive lifelong changes in their health and nutrition. Donna received her training at the Institute for Integrative Nutrition. Through her work, Donna empowers others to find optimal health through nutrition, intuition and self-care. She believes when you are aware of and sensitive to your body's intuitive knowledge, you become aware of the changing conditions in your body and are better able to monitor your health challenges, and nurture your wellbeing. Stay in touch with Donna by signing up for her newsletter to keep abreast of current events, programs, or to work with Donna one-on-one, on her website www.DonnaMarkussen.com.

Made in the USA
Middletown, DE
07 June 2017